ART OF MIND III

THE EVOLUTION OF A TRILOGY

BY ORIGINAL CLYDE AIDOO

ISBN: 0615694349

ISBN-13: 9780615694344

Library of Congress Control Number: 2012948689

Real Print for Real People

This is my story.
This is *our* book.

LAWS OF LIFE

I found a chink
in the
Laws of Life
&
It can't be pried by the
Jaws of Life.

Fertility springs
&
Sunlight sings
from a flower that has
only begun to sprout.
She beams a high
early light like a bright pink rosella prepared to
take flight...

Smacked down
before her prime—
70 years before
her time.

Life can malfunction on even pure, natural things...no one
is exempt...
Wrong Place,
Wrong Time—
It's time:
Daisy's pushing up roses.

I found a chink in the
Laws of Life
&
It can't be pried by the
Jaws of Life.

Beautiful people can do ugly things.
And the right touch could
reform a being:
From a monster of society
to
One of the Beautiful People.

Some remain locked and rehabilitated,
Others are free and uncompromising...
Justice is only seen from the outside,
but what if 80 percent of who we *really* are—

Lies locked—in the inside?

I found a chink in the
Laws of Life
&
It can't be pried by the
Jaws of Life.

Love.
There it is.
You have it,
You hold it.
Until it begins to slip—

Whether or not you choose to let go.
You see, love *is* indeed real, and like all real things:
With time it should perish.
The feeling that reigned through its tenure was no less
genuine or Powerful
just because its royal majesty was forced to take
a step down.
The loves of lives end up a memory in the face of a new
love. Some even have more true loves than they can
count on both hands...not because the loves weren't
real, or because they were easy...maybe they just had
such a tender heart it remained open even when held by
another—strummed by a brand new lover.
The prior owners then accept defeat and so the cycle
continues until the wheel stops on the winner—not based
on the strongest love—
but just the circumstances and life settings that happen
to match in the moment, until
Life ends
or
Loneliness wins.

Then there are those who rule love with a firm authority
appointed by a divine authority for a divine purpose. They
made it work...
They survived...
Until one of them died.

Before then, their names were joined, but how tight did
their bond remain? The answer varies.

After death, how long until the survivor moves on...and dies in another's arms?
And if the survivor remains faithful, waiting to be joined with that One Love in Heaven...
They made it together for 50 years...

Now they just have another infinity to make it last.

I found a chink in the
Laws of Life
&
It can't be pried by the
Jaws of Life.

Desire.
I often wonder what desire—the concept of wanting something with everything within you actually translates to in this world.
It is a concept that I have written about often, and think about even more.
What if the man who wants each individual girl the most was the one who got her? Wouldn't that be a perfect world?

No.

Because it must go both ways. The very same right every man has to dream and hope and desire and love, is the same right every woman (and vice versa) has to desire someone else more...or even not desire you at all.

It's nobody's fault.

Not hers.
Not his.
It's just the facts of life.

So that same desire is then placed in material things:

Fame.
Fortune.
Or even simply a profession to be proud of.

Then the playing field will even, if not tilt in your favor.
And even if you still don't find your love, at least that
profession or the consumers of your fame appreciate
you...because in the end—
We all just want to be *Wanted*

The answers to all of these open-ended issues remain
locked.
Every man may think he has the answers, but none of us
wrote the book.
In the end, for all the unfair, and even untimely and tragic
events, we all try to open up the vault that holds these
answers, while the truth of it all is:
Only One Entity can reveal it.

Yes,
I've found a chink in the
Laws of Life;
No,
It can't be pried by the
Jaws of Life.

Ruffled Clouds Inc. Presents

A Philosopoetic Magic Number Volume

In Association with RPRP Publications

Editing by

Clyde Aidoo
Nick Marco

Chapter 17 Translation by

Anna Perez

Artwork Provided by

Dian Bernardo
Bruce Braithwaite
Claudio Biason

And Featuring the Art of Joy Appenzeller Bauer

Written, Spliced, and Produced by Original Clyde Aidoo

Art of Mind III
The Evolution of a Trilogy

By Original Clyde Aidoo

CHAPTER 1

IT'S READY

It's Ready

It's nights like these when a mother of eight would pray
for more mouths to feed.
The satisfied smiles and filled spirits are rewarding
enough.
Some things you just can't put a price on,
&
Gratefulness covers the Gratuity.

While she feeds that family of eight with a smile on her
face,
She can look back on this night with a sense of
accomplishment.
For in that house,
She's the Top Chef,
And the Master Chef,
Even though Only She knows she went through
Hell's Kitchen to create her masterpiece.

Her sweat, labor, and talent still paid off...just ask the
judges.

There is no pantheon...the title of Iron Chef is reserved for her.

I too may not be serving a wide audience with experts taking the time to objectively evaluate what I serve, but I am still happy to provide selflessly and uncover what I've had dished up for quite some time. I'm not expecting any awards or five-star treatment...only for the few who have joined me—my family—to enjoy. Sustenance isn't always edible...and is received by both provider and taker.
Every single person who comes back for more:
 Is all the motivation I need to get right back to work.

And just as the most generous and fostering of mothers—or fathers—who feed without asking for anything back: I will often hesitate to ask for feedback...

So on behalf of every Mother, Father, and Creator in the World:

I Hope You Like It.

Unwritten

I may feel one way today, and then revert to not feeling a damn thing tomorrow.

I could hold an opinion
Firm & Strong...
And it could still shift like a misinformed amoeba.

I could end up a proud father of three, but be remembered for my tales of loneliness. I could die in a
Blaze of Ecstasy...
And still leave a
Twisted Dark Legacy.

Before you judge me on what you've read...after everything I wrote...

Today is a brand new day...therefore my thoughts remain a
Complete Mystery.

Though I'll be remembered for the little that I did...
Instead of all the aspirations that I didn't...
I could write until my Last Dying Breath,
And my final thoughts will remain
Unwritten.

The Inspiration

When life hands them lemons,
They make Masterworks.
Days that begin as tomatoes—
They grind into Heinz Field.
You see tomato,
They *say* tomato—
But they don't simply say, "tomato,"
but rather, "Fried Green Tomatoes."

This is a world where everyday
Walks of Life
become
Motion Pictures—
Given the right lens.

How can so many seemingly ordinary days inspire so
many proverbs, aphorisms, poems, movies, songs, and
Art
Among So Many People?
It is the different strokes of man that allow aesthetes to
paint such pretty pictures. At this instant the inebriated
lovers who strip art from the aesthetes are inspired by all
too extraordinary days—
Thus it is their works that engulf art the most.

CHAPTER 2

ART OF MIND: PHILOSOPOEMS TO THE
WORLD: THE GALLERY (CONTINUED)

Vivid Dreams

Leave her be.

Don't you

ever wake a mental giant.

If you think one can't dream without eyes closed—

Look Again.

If you think she is before you and not off away deep in

thought—

Think again.

Her eyes are barely hanging on her own weaving words

while her mind is painting structures in clouds high with

soaring birds.

Her introspection draws a melody with a violet and vivid

glisten,

Her wheels are rapidly turning,

all while

She stands in place to listen.

Leave her be.

Her ungrounded earth is filled with patterns

foreign

to you and me.

Her eyes are not parallel to this globe's green static lines—

at first glance her thoughts are beneath it...

but when you stop and

Look Again:

Her mind is Clearly Above It.

Painted by Juliette Caron

The Entrance Sand Bar—New South Wales

Gulls of the sea, voyagers with sons, and experienced sailors are awestruck by this incredible expanse. Their breaths are taken by the panoptic smell of clean air, they marvel at the clear blue water, and they stop to watch the tide wash over the sandbar creating spontaneous shapes that draw a direct map for the senses. However, you do not need to travel out at sea to experience the calm of the water complemented by the fresh green peninsula with golden edges or the steady waves that crash against it. Yes, now you can join them all and explore this incredible view:
All from inside your room.
You don't have to be Abel Tasman or James Cook to navigate this setting to a wide-open vista.
Just pull up a chair, grasp the helm of your mind,
&
Sail Away.
Sail Away.

Painted by Joe Cartwright

Long Hair and Innocence

I saw a young girl in the field today.

She wore a long, antediluvian, almost robe-like light purple dress that went down to her ankles...which were covered by high white socks. She wore brown leather salt-water sandals and she had incredibly long hair tied in the longest and widest French braid I have ever seen. It had to be five inches thick, and went down to the small of her back...held by a thin, light-blue elastic holder. The tail end of her hair went all the way down to her thigh. It's the type of hair that only a young girl could wear. It symbolized her innocence, as did everything about her. I didn't catch a glimpse of her face, but she probably had eyes of bluestone, and perhaps light freckles...

Her back prevented me from seeing the rest of her, but I saw more than just that long hair and innocence. Yes, I could swear I saw fearlessness. The type of bravery and vigilance usually reserved for whiskered grown men and muscle-bound hunters was collected by this Long-Haired Gatherer...
Who stood arranged to protect
Her innocence.

Painted by Debi Watson

8

Castle Doorway

Here in South Suburbia:
You see a Castle,
I see a Cave.
I'm not used to visitors, so I'll be sure that by the time this
door closes:

You'll remember you were here.

Yes, you can come inside...
I have some milk and cookies,
If you decide it's not your taste—
Acknowledge the
Blood, Sweat & Tears
It took me.

You'll witness a creepy museum without masks, but
rather an
Open Heart & a Bared Soul in over 99 broken pieces.

Maybe the nation will join us,
Until then it's just you and me...
Playing these notes for only a few—
Is a
Bittersweet Symphony.

Well, I've left the light on for you:
Venture inside if you'd be so kind.
This is a Celebration of *Art*:

Welcome to Art of Mind.

Painted by Joe Cartwright

CHAPTER 3

SCRAPBOOK

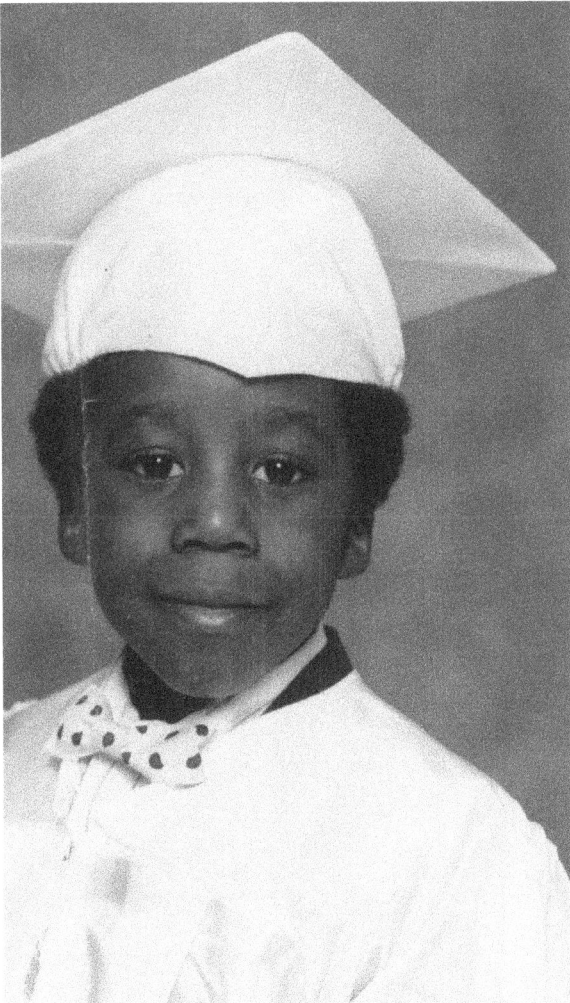

Scrapbook

Precious carats of time cannot be restored—
Not even by
Chips off the Block.
We can only pick up the scraps
and protect this lasting jewel,
Even when the next generation
Falls Apart.

She and He

She wore a trim pink tank top...
That was the color of her nursery five years ago.
They named her Rachel, and she was the newest of
three...a welcomed addition to the
Family.
She holds the brown skin & heart of cinnamon...
Carrying the birthmark of a permanent smile.
Last year she shared her laughter with family and friends,
with her dancing rendition of "Billie Jean" at her birthday
party.

Today she has medium curls with a yellow ribbon.
To the Bennetts she is Li'l Rey-Rey.

Remember the look on Joseph's face when he unwrapped
his Tonka remote-controlled car last Christmas?
The Hansons do. He was the boy who lit Christmas.
His surprise and animation was a gift they'll *always*
remember—with or without the aid of their Samsung
camcorder.

They named him after his great grandfather Joseph—
Lieutenant: 34th Infantry Division.

He has blue eyes and neat blonde hair. He's wearing a
blue polo shirt with playful white stripes along with tartan
shorts.

It's just another day for us as the children gather for this
monumental first day in what is to be the rest of their
lives.
Come recess, whilst concurrently with so many on this
very playground and around the world:
She and He
exchanged stories, joined hands & families:
The very moment that they said,
 "Hi."

The Passage

You may call it a sacrifice,
She will call it a blessing.
A privilege.
One from the
Most Highest.
A blessed occasion to be revisited in an annual reminding
ritual—of a laborious, draining passage—in a glorious rite
of passage.

You must now prepare,
For soon your role will shift,
Until the year arrives
When you return The Gift.

* 誕生祝い*

There are well over 5,000 languages in the world.

Not tonight.

Tonight the same audible cry is heard...

In the:

República Federativa do Brasil,

Jamhuri ya Uganda,

Republiken Finland,

Gumhūriyyat Misral-'Arabiyyah,

Bhārat Ganarājya

Estados Unidos Mexicanos

y

The United States of America...

In hospitals in Lima, Ohio.

The same audible cry is heard as a thousand nations
rejoice:
In their own native tongues:
In a decodable jovial voice.

The entire world will never agree on some things,
Having the same language is certainly one of them. But
ironically, at one point, we *all* expressed ourselves the
exact same way:

At the most crucial point of our lives.

Let us rejoice!
Un Celebración!
For *every arrival* around this world:

A Million Hopes are Born.

CHAPTER 4

CARS

Highlife

It always took just an up-tempo beat to comfort us...

Even if we never understood a word they were saying.

Ah, but those horns and guitars speak a universal
language beyond Twi, and when they sing in English to
bring everybody together: We were already there.

Because these sounds take all listeners to the Motherland,
while introducing America to *kente* cloths and *jollof* rice...
though it always seemed to remain a secret—trapped
in our basements and stuck in our halls. But we didn't
complain. We had each other and peanut butter soup to
die for on a Sunday afternoon and *kenkey* at our mothers'
houses.

If it wasn't Michael Jackson, it was always *these* songs
that served as our background music as we frolicked in
closed-off spaces and took to the races on to our latest
adventure...
Now I can't wait to catch up.

Boy, we were too young to dabble in alcohol,
but we were already drunk on life...
Miller Genuine Draft don't got nothin' on this...

This is Highlife.

Spend the Night

My mother says we can spend the night!
I can't wait!
What a night!
What a night!

Every visit feels like a reunion.
A special family reunion.
Just us six, and it was just last week—
But this is the Perfect family reunion!
I can't wait for us to stay up all night!
And make the most of this Friday night.
Maybe we can even stay till Sunday!
Let's ask our folks if that's all right.
Ooo! First we can play Hide and Seek!
Then flip Uno cards like we did last week.
Finally we can play Nintendo:
That's when the night starts to hit its peak.
Ninja Turtles,
Definitely Mario Brothers,
Some Street Fighter
Then Mike Tyson's knockout—Let's keep playing until we
drop out:
All Night.
All Night.
Tomorrow we can play Tecmo Bowl:
All Day.
All Day.
When it's time to go,
I'll ask to stay...

We still need to watch some
Kid 'n Play —
Then watch
Coming to America—
Just like yesterday.

Either way, we'll see you next Friday...
Just in time for *Full House*...
This was another weekend to remember,
Maybe next week y'all can stay at *our* house!

Buck-Fiddy Grizzled

And Now!!!

Coming down the aisle...

At a Buck-Fiddy Grizzled...

A Grown-Ass Man in the Toy Aisle!!!

<Crowd Goes Silent>

And that's how I like it.

I need the peace and quiet to return to a time when My Mind Went Wild with the roar of a Jam-Packed Crowd.

Whenever I walked down the aisle...
My ring attire was just a massive smile.

Now I'm back not to purchase, but for the purpose of remembering that feeling.

I was usually accompanied by my father down the aisle; ready to wrestle with the grueling task of deciding which figure I should get...

"There are so many possibilities, but I can only get two... though I'd love to have way more...
But we'll be back next Saturday...then maybe he'll let me get four!

Ooooh! I can already imagine who they'll face...and who I'll pit them up against!"

Each Monday, an hour before *Monday Night Raw*, I had my *own* Monday Night Raw: 7 p.m. Central every Monday on the hour. Each meticulous show concluded precisely at 8 p.m., just in time to catch my competition. And once a month, I held my own pay-per-views that literally brought the house down—shattering not records, but upstairs glasses and noise barriers with the vibrations of action and imagination that can only happen
Once in a Lifetime.

Now here we are all these years later;
Instead of a scrawny kid, I'm
100 percent Chiseled.
Now *I'm* a smaller version of these Giants:
Coming in at a Buck-Fiddy Grizzled.

And I'm man enough to return to this aisle.
And I'm still boy enough to again wear that smile.
And I'm still Human enough to never forget:
The smell of this packaged fantasy-land...
&
The feeling of unwrapping its plastic...

Freeing me, them, and this land itself
To roam in a jurisdiction dictated only by me.

I got jitters when I walked down this aisle,
And now the Figure known as "Buck-Fiddy Grizzled,"
Has reverted to the ten-year-old child...

Man, do I miss him.

Windows

When I was a very young boy, my favorite thing in
the outside world was to go out for car rides all day—
particularly on Saturdays. Usually it'd be with my father—
he was an independent courier and he'd be out driving
all day. I was busy with school during the week, but on
Saturdays, I'd ride all day with him...and on more days
in the summertime—sort of like Calogero and *his* dad
in *A Bronx Tale*. Or I'd ride around all afternoon with
my mother on Saturday—running errands and grocery
shopping. Or I would ride around with them both—or the
entire family—with my brother and sister on a night visit
to a family relative, or on a long Sunday afternoon around
town before and after church.

Regardless of the day, time of day, or how many others
in the vehicle—my favorite part about these rides was to
take a backseat to the world—and stare outside of the
windows.

***

I could be the only passenger in the vehicle and still take
the backseat.
And if it was a full ride—while others shouted, "Shotgun!"
I just strolled over to the back door. When it was just me
I loved the extra space, but of course if I was with my
siblings they always had me sit in the middle...those were
the "rules."

Whether I was squeezed in the middle or all alone in the backseat, I loved to prop up against the backseat and stare out the back window or lean against the door with my head tilted to the side looking out into the world. It was all so fascinating to me as a child:
The
Streetlights, the room lights of buildings as towering as John Hancock, or another one of many apartment complexes or homes,
Porch Lights,
Bright Lights,
Headlights,
"All of the Lights."

I've never liked a rainy night,
but from the backseat of your father's sedan—
thunderclouds never looked so bright.

And on a sunny day, the view is Always Moving.

Everything always looked so corresponding and in such harmony. If you ever want to go back and remember the innocence and awe with which a child views the world: look out the back window on a crowded expressway. You don't hear honking, you hear *life*. You see all these hundreds of people learning to share. You see families behind the wheel on a mysterious journey. And if you're lucky, you cross eyes with someone doing and thinking the same as you are. It's a bond that I can still feel decades later—even if I can't remember their faces, I remember the parallel place we found ourselves in that moment—and I still feel each wave and smile.

I'll always treasure those trips with my father—with nothing but us, the radio, those six windows...along with the
Rest of the World.

Cars

Look out of the window with me—
Look at all the many cars:
Small cars,
Big cars,
Parked cars,
Moving cars:
Look at what man and woman built—
This world of rapid high-octane speed that's crowded with
love and raging with lust.
When I look out the window of a train or a landing
airplane—I look at the walking people...and am amazed at
all the
Moving cars.
Every car has a story. The person behind the wheel was
conceived and grew into another driver. Before you know
it you're staring at non-stop traffic—with *individual* stories
of love we know nothing about. We just see another car...
while aficionados care more about the make than they do
the inside model.

I also see crowds of strangers walking on foot...also with
stories from unique contributors.

Each car, and even each hitchhiker or vagrant was built
from scratch not with steel and bolts but with the most
tender parts. Some creations weren't so tender, but these
drivers seem to overcome and keep moving forward...
blending in with all the rest.

We see car after car after car and though we can pinpoint the type and the country it was built in, we know *nothing* about the makers. But we all know that we *need* these contributors...for it is *they* who make the world run.

So many people have the desire to create...
To make their contribution to this running world.
They may have the tools, but lack an assisting partner...or *have* a partner, but lack the required tools.
So they watch life pass from the side of the road—

Looking at what man and woman built.

They can cram inside auto shops across the state—
Fill their garages with paid-off vehicles,

And still hope to someday have their own car.

CHAPTER 5

FAIRY TALES

Fairy Tales

Because there is more to a woman than if she says yes.

Whether a princess or a wicked witch—her story has been written Long, Long Ago, in a land Far, Far from you. These brief moments may call her character into question from *your* balcony—but her sleeping beauty is more than skin deep, and your spell's inability to rouse an Awakening does not disprove that it rests inside her. Whether she has found her prince or is holding out for one, whether she sees a frog while you see Prince Charming, whether you are
Stood Up,
Dismissed,
Or even Ignored—She has love to give—and is *already* loved—by a brother, a sister, or a fairy godmother.

I believe that there is more to a woman than her response.

And there is more to a man than his penis size.
No ruler known to man can measure integrity, values, honor, or a unique sense of humor. Women around the world could see a row of disrobed men and look to reveal what's underneath the package to find the Total Package. He's his own member of society much larger than any comparable member...he stands on his *own* two feet and has his *own* place in the world that should be noticed! I believe there is more to a man than his penis size and bank account. Women can surely see that. There is more

to a woman than whether or not she says yes—I know
deep down my brothers realize that, too.
Ah,
&
I also believe
Love *Always* Prevails,
Yes, I *do*
Believe in Fairy Tales.

People Who Walk Slow in the Wintertime

You know it gets
Cold Outside,
Why do people walk slow in the
Wintertime?

The temperature is frosty and frigid—but is much colder
when you're all alone.
It's too much for me to bear, while I
Power walk—
They don't seem to care.

Then I remembered.

They are blanketed with love, bundled with the thoughts
of a new bundle of joy or his face when he receives his
first
Christmas toy...
They can survive a Chicago Snowstorm,
they have pictures in their wallets to help
Keep them Warm.
Meanwhile I'm unshielded without love's sugar coat
&
Again-Begin the holidays on a
Sour Note.

Oh, how I could use such a *Warm Place*

You know it gets

Cold Inside—

Watching people walk slow in the

Wintertime.

CHAPTER 6

WARM PLACE

Warm Place

She could only hail from such a Warm State.
She always comes from such a Warm Place.

She has the heart of Palm Trees and Sunbeams.
Each Visit is Exquisite.
I want to go with her.
In Chicago,
I'm Always Freezing.

Her warmth takes me So Far North—
It could only be sent from Down South.

Then again, Each Word that blows in this wind
Takes me on a tour through California:
If those are the windows to your soul—
Then Babe, You've got Golden Gate Eyes.

Or she could always move to Tennessee...
Since she's the only Ten I...Blah.

She could only hail from such a Warm State,
I swear
She always comes from such a Warm Place.

And if the day comes when you find you're in the cold,

In My Heart You'll Always Keep A Safe Place.

Angel-Proof Omnipotence

I'm powerful and now I know it;
It took knowing her to empower me
&
Show It.

Now I can do anything.

I can carry the carriage of a dozen stallions.
I can weather the weight of a storm of anchors.
I can spy the sun with gamma-ray goggles.

Hell, I can even listen to a vinyl Donny Osmond record...
On repeat.

Titling her "Angel" paints no clearer a picture for all who
have heard the proverbial term time and time again...even
if I know she's the closest thing to the actual meaning.
And to know and communicate with such an entity on
a regular basis: week after week, day after day, with
no hope, no expectations, and a total abandon of even
fantasizing...

Proves I'm prepared for whatever life may bring,
Befriending an Angel without emotions chasing flight:
Proves
I can do anything.

The Tide that Came but Never Appeared

Wow, you are such a
Beautiful Muse,
Oh, you're coming to visit?
That's Wonderful News.
That knocks me
Out of my Shoes,
A glimpse of an angel?
I'd Hardly Refuse.
This is a dream of
Improbable Views,
An ongoing wish
I'm likely to lose.
Whether or not my
Nearness you choose,
You'll always remain
My sweet, beautiful muse.

Stardust

There's a certain magic in the air.
Of a Virtual Variety.
What we are—I don't know or care to define.
I will protect our secret like an illusionist—No, I won't
touch it. I can't lose it.
I want to drown in our mystery bank—only to emerge once
more unscathed.
I want you to remain the escape artist I admire from afar...
While you feel
Close Enough to Touch.
Satellites from the prairie crash into my big city reveries...
we will remain star crossed—by no plane our paths
cross...only in *this* realm can we dance in the galaxy of
our bayou—because every day is Mardi Gras with you:
You make me bare my chest.
You see those bright lights? Center stage awaits us. You
are a true Dorothy Dietrich. Me? I'm here trying to pull a
rabbit out of a hat. I've heard that we are only allowed to
have three great ones in our lives. Sonny LoSpecchio said
that. But my sleight of hand lacks grace or command, so if
you are the last that I may lose—I dread the performance
of a Hat Trick.
My three great loves were actually three great wishes that
never were. Whenever I tried to work my magic—the clout
disappeared. Even when life fades, the stars remain in the
sky; so you'll maintain your position on my "Wish List." I
envision our stars aligning, and I see fireworks. Yes, I see
cosmic rays of neon lights with our names written all over
them. We'd show out like showgirls, with a panoramic

view of the scintillating starbursts that shine, "Special for you and me." I intend to hold the sparkling glitter of this mental eruption in the palms of my stems... for should this intricate magic that we have worked so hard to master become a reality in which the luster lies in the performance of my clumsy, inept hands...

I am afraid that this glitter will reveal as dust.

CHAPTER 7

DREAM MATCH

The Saddest Love Lamented

Relationships, crushes on a familiar face ending in premature rejection that terminates a one-sided courtship...even engagements that falter before and after the altar...each have completed chapters. There's no need to ask what would happen when you've already finished the book.

Sometimes it's the ones we *wished* to know, who leave the biggest question of what could have been, and whether or not you would have been good together. And sometimes, we only have *one chance* to determine if Love at First Sight really does exist. If that chance is not seized, it remains a case of "You never know."

And if you never see her again, you have to live with it for the rest of your life...maybe that very fact proves:

That love at last sight *is* real.

There she is.

There she goes.
The *one chance* you had—you've blown...
There's nothing like wondering
What Could've Been—
With a girl you've
Never Known.

Somewhere

I do believe there is someone out there for everyone.

There is a woman who can take the weight off
A burdened, oversized man.
A man who can make the most wary woman
Learn to trust again.

A woman who can turn a shy mute
Into the life that makes the party shine.
A man who could make a crippled woman—
Learn to walk Cloud 9.

A woman who won't care what others think—
Even if the whole world says he's too ugly.
A man who cares more about what's *inside*—
When *she* thinks she is short and chubby.

There are men and women
who if found,
Would take their liberties:
To free a tortured soul:
Of all insecurities.

And I believe there is a man for every woman.
There is a woman for every breathing man.
I assure you there *is* someone who'd care,
but for far too many
They are still out there.

Dream Match

Close your eyes
&
Dream with Me.

And together:
Let's ask the age-old question,
"What if?"

What if two people at their *best* could defy time and space
and meet in the middle of the circle? Not the squared
circle, but the blue circle. I'm talkin' bigger than
Tyson vs. Ali,
M.J. vs. LeBron,
Hogan vs. Sammartino,
more magical than
Batman vs. Superman.
And in *this* match—
We wouldn't have to wonder who would win, because it'd
be obvious that they *both* would.
Yes, what if there was a time machine where centuries
and decades could come together for the purpose of
trampling over time limits—to give us our perfect match?
What if 1987's Brian Collins met 1924's Betty Bell?
What if 1996's Andy Turner met 1795's Tina Reed?
What if 2010's Anna Gomez met 1906's Julius Williams?
Some may wonder what if 1955's Marilyn Monroe met
1999's Brad Pitt. But no—you don't have to be famous to
have a Dream Match.

Anybody could create magic—if only they had the chance to meet.

What if our *perfect* match isn't in our beds, schools, or hometowns, but in another generation, era...or another town?

Yes, what if 2013's Chris Wilson from Philadelphia met 2013's Demetria Wells from Kentucky?

These would all make for quite the showdowns, and something would have to give; most certainly it would be two hearts—of which they would so

gladly give.

In return the world would witness a true dream match: years & years already in the making.

"Some may say I'm a dreamer, but I'm not the only one."

So open your eyes now but *don't* stop dreaming:

For yourself, the lonely, and the departed:

To meet our

Match — Made

In Heaven.

CHAPTER 8

GOSSIP

Gossip

Sorry...

I heard...

~   ~   ~

...

I heard the sad news
The other day,
I'm checkin' up,
I hope you're okay...
You'll be better off without him anyway,
I'm just droppin' by to say:

I heard Terrell and Pam
Broke it off,
Four of the best spent years—
Now lost.
He went to chase his dreams at an Ivy League—

Leaving Pam
To bear the cost.
They swore they'd visit often
And write...
Until Pam got a call one night...
It was Terrell and
He
Just
Called to say
That he met someone, and got engaged.
The best four years of her life and the hopes she saved,
Went down the drain
On his wedding day.

Pam sat in her bed and she cried for weeks,
Soaking her tears in all the memories...

To this day she *still* cries...

When her thoughts get lost in her daughter's eyes.

So,
Hold on,
Little girl...
I promise
This ain't
The end of
Your wor-orrld...
There'll be a Hurricane
Jim, Ray, Matt, and Stu
And you'll survive each

Twist & Swir-irrl...

You gotta stoooop
Poutin'...
There's a lot more
Rocky Mountains...
Keep climbin' through
What don't kill you...
And keep enjoyin'
life's grand
Open View...

I heard that tough folks last
but
tough times don't...
I heard that fake friends leave
but
real ones won't...
I heard that when it's bad
It could be much worse;
And remember:

You heard it here first.

~   ~   ~

...

And did you hear about
Ronny White?
The son of great wideout

Bryan White?
Heard he's from the Wide Great Open Engine State
And from his pop
He got his drive.
Every night before they went in...
The sense of long hard work was instilled in...
They played catch then fished,
They worked hard then hitched—
The family wagon out to those
Great Lakes.

One night dinner was hot on the plate...
Mom and Ronny sat up
waiting late...
Then there was a ring of the bell
at the door,
There was a crash on
Route 24...
How could the family survive?
Without the leader who supported them?
A mentor, a supporter, a loving dad:
Is how Ronny would remember him.

Now his mother and his girlfriend Tasha
stand together watching from
row eight...
And every time Ronny runs into the end zone...
For his father:
He celebrates.

So,

Hold on,
Little girl...
I promise
This ain't
The end of
Your wor-orrld...
There'll be a Hurricane
Jim, Ray, Matt, and Stu
And you'll survive each
Twist & Swir-irrl...

You gotta stoooop
Poutin'...
There's a lot more
Rocky Mountains...
Keep climbin' through
What don't kill you...
And keep enjoyin'
life's grand
Open View...

I heard that tough folks last
but
tough times don't...
I heard that fake friends leave
but
real ones won't...
I heard that when it's bad
It could be much worse;
And remember:

You heard it here first.

~   ~   ~

...

You know Elisha?
I heard she got married...
To Derrick Turner and planned a
Family...
They'd have a daughter and name her
Haley...
They couldn't wait, oh they were so hap-py.
It's what Elisha wished her life-to-be.

Until one day Elisha came home...
And found a stranger
in her bed...
With a tear in her eye and a file in her hand,
She looked at Derrick, and then she said,

"I'm Pregnant."

~   ~   ~

...

Derrick and Elisha would then get divorced,
And Haley was well on her way...
She was six months in when the doc slipped in,
Elisha dropped when she heard him say,

"Your baby's gone."

Well, Elisha lay down and cried.
As she would in bed for all the months ahead...
She lay alone and she wondered each night,
How God could let her child be dead.
She thought of Derrick and that mistress, too;
How they made a fool of the life she led...
Until one day it happened:

Elisha got out of bed.

She put one foot in front of the other...
Until one day she found another...

She allowed hope to rise again,
Now she's expecting a baby boy...
And if she ends up having a little girl...
This time she thinks
She'll name her Joy.

And now I know that-that boy hurt you,
And you think there's no way you'll
Get through...
But now if they can get through all of that...
Then little girl, I know you can, too...

So,
Hold on,
Little girl...
I promise

This ain't
The end of
Your wor-orrld...
There'll be a Hurricane
Jim, Ray, Matt, and Stu
And you'll survive each
Twist & Swir-irrl...

You gotta stoooop
Poutin'...
There's a lot more
Rocky Mountains...
Keep climbin' through
What don't kill you...
And keep enjoyin'
life's grand
Open View...

I heard that tough folks last
but
tough times don't...
I heard that fake friends leave
but
real ones won't...
I heard that when it's bad
It could be much worse;
And remember:

You heard it here first.

Not In Attendance; Still Taking Notes

Every relationship there is or ever was—
Has been taken for granted.
Yes, including yours.
Not that You care.
Your love is Solid and Enduring...
It is also rare, special,
&
Especially Unique...
That's all that matters.
Even if you two are the only in the world—
Who fully know,
or
Truly Care,
They aren't here.
They weren't there.

To everyone else you're just two more people holding
hands, walking down the street, sitting in the theater, or
showing PDA.
Many close to you know of your union, and for an instant,
so do onlookers also
In Attendance.
It doesn't matter that they don't seem to care—
They aren't here.
They weren't there.

***

For whatever it's worth: I'm intrigued by your past—and what your future brings,
I know some moments and details are sacred:

But I want to know Everything.

Dirty Little Secret

Ooooo...I'm tell-innng...

I know the dirty little secret...

I'm tell-innnng...

Men are

Fantasized,
Craved,
Desired,
And yes:
Objectified
just as much...
sometimes it's even in plain sight,
but if it's not in a rap video then it's considered all right...

Which it is.
It's only human.
It's natural...
It's a force that can't be amended,
so why is only One Group
always offended?

Athletes and actors may be looked at as Gods...but they are just as human as that girl on the pole...or the girls in that rap video...

And if our catcalls are a bit too loud…it's only because we don't hold them in until we reach the nearest knitting circle.

What results from these secrets is a pedestal of myths, which too many suckers are afraid to climb.

It is the secret that
Everyone Knows,
but is guarded well—
Thus is
Rarely Exposed.

CHAPTER 9

THE GRANDEST LARCENY

Test Drive

Before you make a commitment—and sign your name on
that dotted line,
You need to know what you'll be riding,
You gotta give him a
Test Drive.
I said,
Before you make a commitment—
And sign your name on the dotted line...
You need to find out how she rides,
You must give her a
Test Drive.

You don't want to deal with
Stalls, Malfunctions, and Damaged Goods that can't be
repaired...
After having already invested.
Oh,
but don't let *too* many drive you off the lot—
Because then your value drops.

The Grandest Larceny

I confess: I shoplifted once.
Ironically, what I stole was a wallet.
Though I've always lacked sympathy for wealth chipped:
I must admit—I did feel guilty.

So how would I feel stealing a Whole World?

Do onto others as you would have others
Do Onto You.
There are various
Laws of Life
But my people:
That is the
Golden Rule.

So tell me why is this rotten planet
Filled with so many thieves and wannabe thieves?
Because it's the Only Way to Survive.
It's the Only Way to be happy.

Because every man could be another woman's world:
whether or not he knows it.
And every woman is another man's world: whether or not
he shows it.
Ring or not, Everybody's thoughts revolve around that
One special person…
Maybe a husband, wife, boyfriend, girlfriend, "friend," or
simply a crush…
If you want to have someone to hold:

It's *someone's* dreams you have to crush.

We live in a cold, cold world
When
In order to own a Heaven on Earth:
You Must Steal Someone Else's World.

And they don't even seem to repent.

***

The next time you judge a crooked thief,
Ask yourself:
What would *you* do to survive?
What *have* you done to survive?

CHAPTER 10

GAME OF INCHES

The Look

Perception plays a pivotal part in pinning potential
partners.
What's inside—
They don't know or care,
so
They judge by the clothes
you wear.
Piercings and art paint a better view—
Though everything else is no different than you.

Young Brethren,
Love is a
Game of Inches,
but your odds grow if you
know how to play:
She could be this-close to looking at you,
You might just be
One Earring Away.

The Romantic

- Look Deeply Into Eyes
- Speak Sincerely Without Presentation
- Be Yourself and Make her *feel* your Urgency:
These: are the ways—I thought to win—the girl.

The soul of a Romantic is often tamed or defeated by an opponent that may look narrow but is much larger -- Goes much Deeper.
Natural Chemistry and Congenial Spirits may win out, but son, it's a 12:1 Underdog.
This life ain't always a box of roses,
so before you hand one out—ask yourself if it belongs in this world.
In the end, each damsel is different,
But on some things—it seems—you can depend:
- Make her feel *Alive*
- Stimulated
- Enthralled:
These: are the ways—that you can win—the girl.

More than Words

She's gonna make someone happier than words.
But I won't tell her that...
Nor should he.

The most poetic sentiments are felt, not said. It courses
deep inside more potent than any series of three words he
could ever say or any verse I could write.
She in herself is More than Words—Molded in us what
she's never heard.
Now I've already said too much. And if you too must tell
her how you feel:
Tell her in your eyes,
Show it in your touch.

Game of Inches

Distance & diction dictate the determinate in deciding
dates.
Who you are—
Is based off today,
so
they judge by the words
you say.

The most vital things in life are determined by where you
are:
Children, marriage, a family, and love...
Are Out of Reach
If you're
Too Far.

It all begins with that date.
Any guy could win if he brings his
A-Game...
Any Given Guy
can
win
Any Given Girl
on
Any Given Day.

The word "any" is a gross exaggeration.
OK, maybe that's not close at all...
But it's true that performance matters,
It's how you Run your Mouth when you

Have the Balls.

The wrong lines bring in
The Replacements.
When you could have done better tomorrow.
In the end it's about inches and timing,
A man can't find what he cannot follow.

Love is about Home Field Advantage:
Where you are.
Where they are.
Then about timing and delivery,
Don't Trip Up:
You won't get far.

So dedicate this date to little Junior,
Your performance holds his life in your hands...
There are so many players she can choose,
And if you Drop the Ball—then you're left with
Your Hands.

And should you make it to the bedroom:
You
Best Believe
It's a
Game of Inches.

Inches: Distance.
Inches: Word Fragments.
Inches: Love—
Decided by a determinate as diminutive as a stud.

My Brethren,
Love is a
Game of Inches,
but your odds grow if you
know how to play:
You could be this-close to getting the girl,
You might just be
One Earring Away.

CHAPTER 11

ALTERNATE ROUTE

Let it Flow

Let it Snow.
Like a Northwestern winter cool night.
Like a flake that takes and sets flight.
Let it Flow.

Let it Pour.
Like a temperate grey autumn day.
Like a bolt that charges on God's say:
Let it Roar.

Sometimes what hovers is heavier than any cloud,
Unlocking combinations set to meet crowds—
Open Up.

When the log is placed and your words get stuck,
When the pressure builds and feels like too much:

You still can let your nature take course:

Just let it flow.

Alternate Route

Ready.
Set.
Pow!

Off they go.
Others only hear the sound
Of a Gun,
Before
They have a chance to Run.

Don't expect any gasps
from the crowd,
Unless it's from the shock and dismay
of learning how far behind you are.

They don't want to hear it, just
get back up. If you've been left for dead—
Get Stitched Back Up.
Those numbers with the slashes are the starting point, so
you better keep up with the rest.
Seems that when you're running behind:

They're quick to call you a loser,
Even when the race ain't over.

Well,
I say:
Set your own pace, just don't bow out,
Keep right on Charging,

Just don't Foul Out.

You may have to change directions after
Stumbling along the way,
But keep on moving forward:
Another Day, Another K.

And before the race is over,
After everyone has counted you out,
You'll catch up or maybe end up ahead—
With the Late Bloomer's
Alternate Route.

CHAPTER 12

GROWING PAINS

You Wouldn't Understand

Don't look at me.
Not if you won't understand.
You don't know where I've been.
You don't know who I am.
Yet you judge me on your own warped standards.
I don't want to be you.
And I don't wish to look like him.
So no, you don't look at me.
Now I'm convinced that you will *never* understand.

***

My awkward teenage bones hold something larger than
your hateful words and shallow insights.
I am not too black.
I know that I am not ugly.
This black that you call "burnt..."
My Mirror & I know is beautiful.

To anyone being put down by the appointed "beautiful":
If *that* ugliness constitutes as beautiful,
Remember Da Champ said
You are Beyond Beautiful.

Ducklings will blossom in the eyes of someone special who
will understand,
and bodies grow, and so do ideas...yes, you *will* be
someone special...
but you must believe *now* that you were *always* special.

No, don't look at me.

Not unless you can learn to understand.

Growing Pains

Growing up I always enjoyed watching opening credits. Half the time I wouldn't even watch the episode...I just loved the opening credits. I often wouldn't even be a fan of the show...but that didn't stop me from making sure I tuned in at the top of the hour. There were always those programs that had the grooviest theme songs, set to cozy, customized clips.

Everybody has their own favorites...well, at least I know I have mine.

***

My first memory of breaking units of a day's minutes down to a single memorable one was on a late Chicago mornight at about 3:30 a.m. I had to be no older than four. It was in a snug neighborhood basement during a sleepover. I awoke in the middle of the night and the television was still on. *M*A*S*H* was just coming on, and to this day I pause when the theme plays. The images of helicopters, wide grassland and core-cadenced camaraderie always carry me away...to a much more peaceful place.

Maybe I had just turned five. Maybe it wasn't the basement, maybe it was upstairs. Maybe it was 11:30 p.m., not 3:30 a.m. Maybe I was sitting in the room with someone else. The setting is still a bit of a blur, but the one thing that is clearest to me is how I felt in that one minute. I've always felt such a strong connection with that opener. It made me feel like I was one of the soldiers. And yet still to this day: I have never seen a full episode of *M*A*S*H.*

It's the same way with the *Golden Girls.* I've only seen a few full episodes, but I still remember the first time I saw its opening credits. It was a late Saturday night and me and my two older siblings had just finished watching *WWF Saturday Night's Main Event* on NBC. The next thing on was *Golden Girls.* This time I was about six. I swear I even remember the commercial that came on before the show started: *Popeye's.* Then those credits played. In all the passing years since that night, if I was aware of an episode airing on Lifetime, I was right there along with all the various women in America... well, for the first minute anyway.

The opening credits of so many sitcoms are like a hospitable welcome, meant to make us viewers feel right at home—so cozy that we feel like we are actually *part* of that fictional family.

Diff'rent Strokes was meant to open our minds,
The *Cheers* Theme was to help us unwind...
Gimme a Break's left us waiting for more,
And *Taxi's* theme let our souls explore.

And they all did it by getting us hooked before the damn show even started.
Sometimes I'd watch credits like *Taxi's* and wonder if I was the only one noticing that for comedy shows, some of

these series chose really beautiful themes. *Nick at Nite* was always such a soothing way to wind down a weeknight... even if it lasted for less than a minute.

My favorite simple pleasure....my favorite *escape* was to watch many of these programs on a Saturday afternoon. Such as *Diff'rent Strokes*...but it always felt like it was the opening credits that made me feel the most at ease when home alone, or at least alone in the room. *Laverne and Shirley* was the show that made me aware of that Saturday afternoon feeling. When the reruns would air on Channel 50 here in Chicago, it felt almost like a guilty pleasure for a TV show opening to make me feel that good...like it was my little secret or something. During the part when Laverne and Shirley are in the factory, daydreaming about Lord knows what, I find myself equally as invested in the credits as they are uninvested in their work. Since then, my Saturday afternoons were made by relaxing to credits that I may not have even thought twice about if I had seen them on any day but a mellow Saturday afternoon. Shows like *Mr. Belvedere*, *The Nanny*, *Family Ties*...every TV opening suddenly felt like home— on a Saturday afternoon. When it came to the rest of the week, especially Friday nights and openers of the '90s— nobody could match those *Perfect Strangers*.

As for the '80s, though, it always seemed like when it
came to TV theme Perfection, if only one
Got it Right—
It was prolly
The Facts of Life.

Then, there was *Who's the Boss*. Watching that blue van cruising down the road, then Tony, Angela, and the rest of the gang messing around with those New York wide smiles set to that smooth voice and blending flute was just what the house ordered. Far too often something so mundane was a weekend highlight. Sure it was fine as a kid, when I'd revolve my Saturdays around watching *Saved by the Bell* and inwardly coasting to my favorite Saturday afternoon opening credits ever, *California Dreams*, but as an adult? Watching *Who's the Boss* rerun marathons enhanced by the opening credits should not by any means be a weekend highlight...I know that. By no later than 16 it should be going out on dates, bowling, seeing movies, living life! But...Who's the Damn Boss?

Sometimes it feels like I'm trying to make my own show out in the real world and pick a theme song together with someone else...and maybe we could even make a video.

But it feels like I'm pitching a pilot to potential takers... and no one wants to pick me up...or like I want to do a casting call...but I don't know where to start—since I have no connections.

So now, like all these shows...the years keep on ticking away...and my life is still in reruns.

A childhood pleasure when everything was so simple has carried over into adulthood when I now know what else is out there. TGIF Fridays and Sitcom Saturdays were supposed to turn into Party Fridays and Date Night

Saturdays. Instead, those credits rolled on through high school and simple pleasures still tame adulthood.

High School Saturdays were tough...but if I only saw *one* opening video that entire day, it meant that even though 23 hours and 59 minutes of my Saturday may have been unresolved, the other minute would take an empty house and make it feel like a home...and then like any welcoming open door, like any great TV series we all loved, like any classic episode, and like any video of Opening Credits: My day closed.

CHAPTER 13

THE CAPTIVE 48-MONTH DAYDREAM
LABELED "WASTED YOUTH"

Sides

Take Sides.
Then take cover.
Command your Surroundings
And warn adjutants of opposed troops.
Shield the fort that your team has built
From
Wannabees
&
Turncoats
And always be on the lookout for
Fifth Columnists.
There is a security in these arms, but
Everybody knows that the same colors doesn't always
Shade Traitors.
Capture that Flag,
Fling Paint at Whoever Gets in Your Way...
They say the rules are clear,
But out here—the truth is—

Anyone can be Eliminated,

At Any Time.

Choose your disguise wisely to get you through the
competition.

In four or eight years, when it's over, you can remove
that mask covered with paint and take off that [1]*Apatetic
Coloration...*

Until the next time the partners that remain come calling:
And you wear the mask again.

---

[1] Apatetic Coloration — Protective natural camouflage less visible to predators.

$$* \quad d = \sqrt{(x_2 - x_1)^2 + (y_2 - y_1)^2} \quad *$$

There she goes.
Right on schedule.

I've got her timing down to a formula, and my neck snaps
every time she passes by...
I think that's the Reflexive Property.

If she were in my class, then maybe I could actually
concentrate...

Nah.

I'd only break her shape down to each complex fragment.
I'm lost.
I want to get in her box, but I bet she's already in a love
triangle...and she'd prolly think I'm too square to be in her
inner circle.

Well, I'll just keep on sizing her measurements,
I know I should pay more attention, but I don't care—why
lie?
I can't decipher all this hard geometry...
Not when
I'm still stuck on π.

The solution to the problem of all this distance is proving
to her that we'd make congruent complements. Now I

gotta wait another week for this equation to apply...or at least for another chance to *Imagine*

While everyone in class is copying the teacher, I'm here doing my *own work*:

It's 10,080 minutes until our points meet again—
for just another 5 Seconds.

Multiple Choice: So Leave it Open-Ended

Sometimes being gun-shy isn't due to the fear of pulling
the trigger...
but because you're constantly readjusting your aim.

Because Ms. Right Now could become Mrs. Wife:
When if you waited longer you could've Wifed Ms. Right.

So don't approach half-cocked when you don't know who'll
be passing:
If she says yes while Ms. Right just walked away:
You solve the question,
"What's the harm in asking?"

The Captive 48-Month Daydream Labeled "Wasted Youth"

Gagged:
I recall.
Bound:
I felt that much.
Detained:
Jailed without chains.
The rest is a blur
and that's what
I prefer.

Not a single hour went by that I didn't have my bell rung.
So excuse me if it's all a little hazy.
I see red and white Vikings.
This isn't real.
I see a marching band of cliff divers.
They can't be real.
I've already aced the crash course in "who cares,"
Wake me when it's over.
I'm channeling the kindred teen spirits of Kurt Cobain,
Dave Grohl, and every other misguided misfit to my own
world: a creative Nirvana.
I'm only beginning to waste this youth,
You can keep the gown,
Just turn me loose.

Exit Dream Street.

Welcome Real World:

Smack dab in the middle.

I'm lost

with

No Direction...

But I'm free.

I'm Free.

CHAPTER 14

THE DANCE

End Result: Lose-Lose

If you're nice, but see the incompatibility—
That's a sure-fire way to come off as stuck-up.
If you're straightforward and simply uninterested...
You'll then be viewed as a bitch.

All they see is the End Result:
In the end—You didn't let him in.
And no matter how delicate or direct:
In the end—You just can't win.

So step carefully as you answer this question:

Will you go to *The Dance* with me?

The Dance

It is a decorated stage to be recorded in the memories
of Mothers and Daughters,
The Wealthy and the Impoverished—
To capture these moments—one need not own a
camcorder:

You Only Must Be in Attendance.

Witnessing the timed steps of history worn
as a garnished corsage with a tender hand
passed down from partner to
partner as the clock continues to roll,
It is important for the participants to remember:
The Music Never Stops...
Even After You've Departed.

So while you're here:
Take the Floor.
Don't wait for a nod—Jump Right In
and *Move* with the finesse of Fred Astaire.
Waltz like Alex Moore,
Slide and Split, Man, like James Brown,
&
Spin, Kick, Shuffle, Moonwalk...
Mmm—*I Wish I Could Dance Like Michael Jackson*
Yes, so do millions of others, but even if
You're not born with
Many extravagant talents and always seem to
show up alone,

You're Still a Part of It.
So *Watch*—Watch the rhythm of others
and those who inspire many to
find their groove:
Some with Golden Voices,
Others with Magic Moves.
Watch them—
And the World—
Continue to
Spin
&
Spin.
The next set may be
More tailored for you than your favorite playlist,
But You May No Longer Be In the Building.
This Dance and Moments of this time—Our Time—
Are treasures that sadly, billions cannot be a part of.
Not because they don't want to.
Not because they did not have a spot reserved.
But only because they're late.

CHAPTER 15

BALANCE

Sign

Jay's BBQ Potato Chips—
2/$5
Only we are too busy trying to read each other.

We both roam about this aisle—
But neither is making a move.

I feel the tension as strongly as the Peach Snapple that's
in my hands,
but without such a touch—I can't be sure...
I feel that She Too is seeking confirmation of a potential
barter...
But what if she really *is* reading the ingredients of Chef
Boyardee?
Maybe we're just another two random people placed next
to one another...
but This, She, & I-Pray-Me-To-She:
Sure does feel special.

Though I can't be certain: I *feel* our dire advertisement—
We Read:
"*Show* Me You Feel This;
Give Me a Sign."

Balance

Mmmm...I hear music.
The clit-clat of her feet
is
as polished as
Beethoven's sheets.
Now my mind's runnin' like soccer cleats...
but I slow down to take the time
to
Listen.

Mmmm...Brava.

It's Beautiful.
Each developed line. Each euphonic measure.

She's got Balance.

She's much more complex than A-Flat.
She's got C-Majors,
With the touch of a baby grand.

She is a cadenza of a faultless bravura with crisp legato
movements.
Hell, she's playing *my* heart like a piano...

Here comes the Crescendo.

I hang on to Every Part,
Not just her moving form.

While others are only keyed in on her body...
They forget that she's got soul:
And it is a Masterpiece.

Bellissima

More for Me

Tonight she told me that she's gained a few pounds...
Then I felt like doing backflips.
Not because there's "more of her to love..." but because
there's now *less* for the world.

So Bon Appétit!
Have some more Po' Boys!
Help yourself to some Chicken & Dumplins,
Biscuits and Gravy and Pecan Pie!
Keep loading up on turkey and jambalaya...stuff yourself
with more stuffing, oh, and of course: Jelly Donuts!
What's that? You've got a craving for some more banana
pudding??
Yes, Please!!
And when you're done with all of that, I got a full slab of
BBQ Ribs with your name on it!

The more pounds—The Merrier!
She could be 5 Bills
&
I'd *still* marry her!

While everybody says she's not their taste,
I'll eat her up and thank the Lord with stuffed face...
While she may change and morph into a different size,
She has the same soul
I craved in the first place.

CHAPTER 16

SUPERMASSIVE BLACK HOLE ABLAZE

Supermassive Black Hole Ablaze

Your Effigy is my Muse
And it Ignites as I
Light the Fuse.

My affection was carved in stone—
It was a monument
Beloved—to Behold...
Now the world is watching it burn.
Burn, baby, burn.

***

S-B-H is my Muse
And it Ignites when they
Light the Fuse.

Electricity breaks out the gate
With Superstar-Static Riffs.

What results is an outer galaxy beat
Exploding from a Neutron Star Collision.

Q: If neutrons have no charge, then how can theirs set my
soul alight?

A: It's out of this fucking world.

Recycled Lyrics

We may not be able to share one another's *Headphones*
But I think I know what you meant.
You may say,
"That was a great song,"
Time after Time,
Since there is
No Art Known to Man
That is harder to capture in words than Song—
Until you just run out of adjectives.
We'll have to rely on the singers to do the talking for us.
We are, after all, sitting right next to one another; and yes,
it's evident to me that those chords spoke to the both of
us.
Just as some lyrics may be recycled, your words have
surely been spoken by you and millions of others over and
over again. And just as with the singer, although you and
I may not realize it, when you say those words, I too feel
the individual pitch of your words that connect you to that
specific song...just as that song connected us.
It goes without saying how great that song was. And I
know you said those same words three songs earlier, but I
can hear the difference. I know what you meant.
The truth is, all we have are educated guesses. I know
where that song took me, and by the stillness of the room
and in our composures, I'm fairly certain where it took
you. And those five words will have to do as the only proof
to validate what I already knew: That Song Speaks for
Itself.

Dancing in the Moonlight

I think I always hear stars when that song starts.
Or, I don't know, maybe I see them, too.
Feels like I'm just plain *in* the stars.
Right up there.
Dancing in the Moonlight.

***

<Set to the Melody of "Dancing in the Moonlight" by King Harvest>

You light my soul
To another Height,
You make me feel so
Out of Sight,
I'm somewhere off on an orbit flight:
You got me
Dancing in the Moonlight.
Dancing in the Moonlight,
You take me
Through a Sparkling Site,
I'm up here Dancing in the Moonlight,
You really
Grooved my Soul To-ni-ighhht

***

A Smooth Baritone Voice
Is just All-right,

Feels this song was played

For

Me

To-night,

But someone else is sharing with me tonight,

And together we're

Dancing in the Moooonlight.

Dancing in the Moonlight,

You take me

Through a Sparkling Site,

I'm up here Dancing in the Moonlight,

You really

Grooved my Soul To-ni-ighhht

Dancing in the Moonlight,

It's a super–

Spiritual Delight,

We're up here Dancing in the Moonlight,

Everybody Feels so Warm and Bright.

I Want to Stay Here

You know, sometimes I think about the moments couples share.
Private moments. Intimate moments. Innocent moments.
Moments that nobody else knows about but them.
Occurring right at the peak of their love. The simple things that build up until they swap rings.
Moments like a young, loving couple underneath the covers, looking out into a blanket of snow...either nestling in front of a fireplace or simply cuddled without a word being spoken...only smiles.

I don't know, I guess this is dedicated to anybody who has had these special moments...but more than that it's dedicated to anybody who is having one right at this very moment...but above all, it's dedicated to any couple who heard "I Want to Stay Here" by Steve Lawrence and Eydie Gormé on the radio in 1963 or any year after that, like 1973...I've always thought the '70s were probably filled with special moments.

If you have such a love, be it a young love or a lifelong mate,
I encourage you to play this song during one of your simple, private, cozy moments.

It'll take you from the '60s to the arms of today,
And you'll share the same moment as great loves of yesterday.

***

I just want to stay here and listen.

CHAPTER 17

INTERNATIONAL GODDESS

International Goddess

She's got the face of a kitten...with the eyes of a Wolf.

She has the lips of a kissing fountain,
&
The voice of a tidal wave...
With the movement of a Spanish Tsunami.

She's got the hair of a Colombian Vixen...
with
The body of an International Goddess.

Anybody who uses the phrase,
"She's the most beautiful woman I've ever seen..."

Is conveniently forgetting about Shakira.

That is the unbiased truth
because
Those Hips Don't Lie...
So don't even listen to me,
Listen to the music of her bodily motion,
& attend to the rhythm of her metaphysical beauty.
Because her outer beauty mixed with her inner beauty...
Has me convinced that she's from another realm. For
years she's belly danced across so many countries right
into our homes, with the sweet disposition that makes
souls dance...
While our hearts skip another beat.

It's a beauty that unites the French Alps, North America,
Portugal, Spain, New Zealand, Ecuador & Africa...
with
China, Australia, Jamaica, Japan, South America—going
back
to
Colombia.

She sings with the language of love so that the Whole
World can understand,
But when she moves I find myself so mesmerized:
Her grace is All I comprehend.

She is the very portrait of
The Art of a Woman
&
The very embodiment of a global beauty.

Can't you see, people, this is perfection.

The music takes us on a caravel cruise—
Let's Tango:
And venture to a moonlit getaway
Underneath Our Clothes:
With the ballads of a Goddess
Taking us Away.

Diosa Internacional

Ella tiene la cara de una gatita... con los ojos de una Loba.
Ella tiene los labios de una fuente de besos,
y
La voz the una marejada...
Con el movimiento de un Tsunami Español.
Ella tiene el cabello de una Zorra Colombiana...
Con
El cuerpo de un Diosa Internacional.
Cualquiera que use la frase,
"Ella es la mujer mas bella que he visto..."
Se olvida convenientemente de Shakira.
Esa es la verdad imparcial
Porque
Esas caderas no mienten...
Entonces no me escuchen a mi,
Escuchen la musica de la moción de su cuerpo,
& asistan al ritmo de su belleza metafisica.
Porque su belleza exterior mezclada con su belleza
interior...
Me han convenzido que ella es de otro reino. Aun—
ella baila la danza del vientre a traves de tantos paises
directamente a nuestros hogares, con la dulce disposición
que hace bailar nuestras almas...
Mientras nuestros corazones saltan otro ritmo.
Es una belleza que une Los Alpes Franceses, Norte
America, Portugal, España, Nueva Zelanda, Ecuador y
Africa...
Con
China, Australia, Jamaica, Japan, Sur America—volviendo

a

Colombia.

Ella canta con el lenguaje de el amor para que el mundo
entero pueda entender,

Pero cuando ella se mueve me encuentro tan hipnotizado:

Que su gracia es todo lo que yo comprendo.

Ella es el mismo retrato de

Arte de una Mujer

y

La misma personificación de una belleza global.

No pueden ver, gente, esto es perfección

La musica nos lleva a un crusero de carabelas—

Vamos a bailar el Tango:

Y aventurar a una huida iluminada por la luna

Abajo de nuestras ropas:

Con las baladas de un diosa

Llevandonos a todos lejos.

Listen

Shhh...put down your *Ego* and listen:
To the Art that is
Beyoncé's "Listen."

Listen.
When a Goddess is singing to you.
Listen to a ballad that is
Larger than Sex,
Arranged for an audience of this nation and hundreds of
others who take to this icon. This is the story of her inner
journey. Of her dreams, her determination, her
Passion.
You better listen.
Because this is a once in a lifetime performer.
Like Ella Fitzgerald, Dinah Washington and Billie Holiday
before her:
Someday she will be gone.
So Listen.
Listen to this song in her heart...
A melody she completed...
After owning it from the start.
She has honed her craft since the age of five...to be
Heard...not pushed aside...or warped into just another sex
symbol
whose Godly talent is immaterial.
No!
She created another masterpiece, and whether it's five
years, ten years, or thirty years later, you *will* Listen. And
you *will* Watch.

She is singing for *every* female performer who has been
held back or underrated...
So you damn well are gonna listen.

Watch
This woman who was once a
Child with a Destiny
and now embraces it not only in her powerful, balanced
voice, but in her
masterfully planned moves every time she takes the stage.
Watch
This cinematic video about a woman who would not
be denied her *own* greatness, but instead rose above
everything and everyone who held her down to claim
a greatness that Diana, Aretha, and Gladys before her
worked so hard to reach.
You should have known!
That stage is a symbol of the destiny she lit!
This "may very well be her best...
Though not on her greatest hits!"
Watch!
The motion, dance, and emotion of a once in a lifetime
performer who's telling her story to you—not to be
forgotten, not for you to search for any flaws, but only for
you to
Listen.
So Watch.

Raise Your Glass

Mariah is the Greatest.
She sets the standard for every vocalist
Past, Present, and Future.
There are others who sing louder and stronger...
But none with the same loveable charm.
Christina channeled that same focus to answer the call of
her idol,
and Pink just keeps getting better and better. Raise your
Glass and toast to her remarkable career.
Madonna is the Greatest.
She sets the standard for every performer
Past, Present, and Future.
Gaga channeled that energy to bring us the same show-
womanship that Madonna did, but in a brand new
innovative way. She embraces the Fame she earned so
quickly.

And who can forget Whitney Houston? Who *made* the tone
for so many of this era.

Or the Superwoman voice of Alicia Keys: That is leading
the way for the next generation.

Let's Raise our Glasses to the women from this Twenty-
Year Era—Arguably the Greatest Female Era.

CHAPTER 18

ART OF MIND II: ALL IN: THE GALLERY

The Look of Love

She's dining in the company of a very lucky gentleman—
who is currently not present.
She's dining in the memory of a fine, distinguished
gentleman—
Who is privileged to be this lady's companion.

They have entered Le Café d'Amour
In spite of their Reservations.
Now, as she awaits her beau,
She's already dining for two.

Patrons and couples notice this damsel sitting by herself...
and it may seem that she is alone...
Do not be fooled by an empty seat:
A Woman Like This is *Never* Alone.

She has eyes that sparkle like crystal chandeliers,
A mane of luscious curls that dangle with her pale green
earrings,

Succulent lips that speak of excursions to Paris—
With a silent expression that's sealed with a kiss.

Messieurs,

Set aside your menus for a moment,
And Feast Your Eyes on a Dish.

Overindulgence will blind you to her beauty, as deep
pain is felt from staring at a radiance of this volume for a
prolonged span.
And before your date becomes wise to his or her own
deficiency—
It's best that you look away.

After all, she only has eyes for one.
And as she awaits his arrival—
It's plain to see that he is already with her.

His presence is written all over her face;
It reads: "Le Regard d'Amour."
And when he finally arrives...
He will be seated by the
Maitre d',
and greeted by the
Look of Love.

Painted by Dian Bernardo

On a Hot Tin Roof

She's so uptown fly she'ont need
Aviation Classes.
She's so smokin' tan cool she'ont need
Couture Sunglasses...

Fit this airshow pilot with some goggles and strapped
galoshes,
And Watch her Take Off.

***

Her proximity to the sun helps forecast why she's so damn
hot.

We're in the middle of a whipstall, while she's poised both
feet on a hot tin tile:

Vogue.

Travelers are moving undercover to try & spy a way to love
her:

Rogue.

They're on Her Majesty's Secret Service.

She's got the Built Frame of a Model Air Plane—
A Hot Rocket Too Fly for Any Terrain.

If you want to see this Stunning Observation...

First, you must get on her level.

She remains steadily in place

to halt

A Crash-Land-Falling from Grace.

She was even sure to Strap Protection on her Kitty-Kat...

Safety First.

You've purchased a ticket to a rousing exhibition;

Though you can't fly with whom you can't see,

&

Her Swag Exceeds a Thousand Degrees.

She travels alone and has already parked on the roof,

Yet we still Marvel at this Stellar Air Display.

Painted by Vincent Cacciotti

No Answer

I've been planning a ghost hunt for Kindred Spirits—
Instead I fell into a preoccupancy.
From a distance I saw a raised flag—
With no one to hail to it,
There was a 90 percent chance of calm—
but
Then the hail blew it.

What soon followed were strong gusts of wind and
paranormal radioactive frequencies that ran cold chills to
the base of my spine.
My head faced the Northeast—in the direction of what
were now two flags...
Then I noticed her Southern Exposure.

On my EVP I could identify a nearly inaudible cry for help.
My hunt turned into a rescue mission.

The voice sounded like that of a young girl—within the
range of adolescence and approaching adulthood. As I
moved forward, I saw a shape grow larger...and this was
no adolescent. It was a form too real to be a specter, too
hypnotizing to be imagined.

I drew closer, now within feet of this phantasm...her back
was turned to me, and she has remained motionless
throughout. Nevertheless, my motion sensors detected a
potential divider, and as I continued to approach, to the
left a young female shadow flashed.

Then Remained.
Then a wraith emerged over on the right,
but just as soon vanished.

My delta rhythm has time-warped me as a visitant to this
magenta capital...haunted by young and lonely spirits.

At Last I reach the Governess.

A puff of cloud-smoke surrounds our ankles, then
condenses into lukewarm water. With her back still facing
me, I gently moved in.
Without the aid of an EMF, I was able to pick up on the
fact that she was naked—so vulnerable. Left bare to face
the grim winds that now softly blew her hair forward.
The hail has long since stopped and we are now left with
only an ominous blue landscape. Together we stand
before a low platform as we both are firm in place. Then,
as I finally spoke to her, I could hear my voice echo
throughout this void:

"What is this?
Where am I?
How did I get here?
When did you arrive?
Please, look at me, tell me:
Who are you?"

She remained silent

as

We planned our escape.

Painted by Chet Davis

Wantonness

They wanted to see All of her—
But she insisted on wearing a mask.

Underneath this masquerade—
Lies a Veil of Shame.
Beneath this wanton display—
Reveals a slight disgrace.

She looks completely uninhibited,
While trapped inside a box.

Welcome to the Raree-Show.
Containing a merry-go-round of gentlemen who are lubed
for a Freak Show.
She attracts a Ferris wheel of jockeys,
because
She is built like a Bouncing Mare.

Hop on Up.

Swing with plated gold cloaks and hang on for an Erotic
Thriller.
Behold the Maiden in Black.
Presenting a leather corset that stops shy of her robust
busts;
Leather & Lace, oh, Leather & Lace,
With a piano key choke that strings the crowd along.
As her presence dominates the room,
She submits to the closing pressure...

She openly welcomes all comers,
Yet continues to hide from her own shadow.

Arrive dressed in your finest white tie,
Listen as the Toms praise, "Magnifica!"
Step Closer &
Imagine fucking her till she's Venetian Blind:

Just don't look at her.

Painted by Vincent Cacciotti

CHAPTER 19

ALL-IN

Release Date

Art of Mind II: All In
Release Date: March 3, 2012
Real Print for Real People

And so it begins.

The anticipation of gamers waiting weeks for the
advertised release of the latest game in their favorite
series,

Ardent movie buffs closing in on that long awaited
weekend.

Sports fans awaiting the day of the big game or big
primetime pay-per-view fight to finally arrive.

Those jitters are shared by millions—when the calendar
just won't move fast enough.
And when the day arrives—boy, when it arrives—
The chills make you feel so alive.

Whether a cult following or a wide legion:
Even if it is a letdown, the impact was already felt.

I may or may not be alone in this line, but I know this is a
big freaking deal.
OK, maybe not to the rest of the world—
but
Dammit, it is to me.

So I guess that begs the question:

If the impact of a release is enormous, and felt with the
same quaking anticipation by *only one person:*

Does it make a noise—
When it Drops?

All-In

When life seems to leave you short-stacked, the only thing left to do is go
All-In.

***

What's lost is lost.
And when the writing is on the wall, why chip away? Even a hot streak will only get you back to where you started. To be fortunate enough to have just enough...not in the bank but in the tank...to dig deep into your pot...in the root of your guts, and sacrifice whatever it is you have and let it all ride, even when you know that failure means elimination.
I'll push in every penny I have for this opportunity.
I'll leave nothing up my sleeve—save maybe one or two
Veins
I'll give everything I have financially, mentally, and spiritually...
Not for any big payout,
but for the opportunity to know
That should I lose,
Should I perish without anything to show for it,
Without any value to my name whatsoever,
I can rest knowing
That I took what I was dealt,
I looked you all bravely in the eyes,
And without fear, prejudice, or reservation,
I was fortunate enough to say,
"All-In."

Empire Prologue

I will take these two hands and with
cracked, then bloody knuckles:
I'll build you an empire—
&
Then I'll retire.

Empire

I will take these two hands and with cracked then bloody
knuckles I'll build an Empire.
I will build a fortress out of rubble,
I'll wear myself down to a stubble.
I will then make an autonomous list:
Then I will rule
with an Iron Fist.

***

This is My Empire.
It is my own.
From *My* Blood,
My Sweat,
My Struggle and hard work,
My Great Black Sea
from a body of hurt.
Intellectual compromise is forbidden—
I dictate law,
And so it is written:

1. What I say—Goes.
2. What I think—Flows.
3. Every line *must* be real.
4. Thou shalt not steal.
5. I shall write from a pure-driven place.
6. One who writes for money shall be ruled a disgrace.
7. Vain motives will result in shame.

8. Thou shalt not write in pursuit of fame.

9. Unoriginal work is the Ultimate Sin.

10. I vow to *always* go All-In.

I welcome
Any Gender
Any Race
Any Creed:
This palace was not built
on Greed.

Even if it *must* be in order to endure.

Every emperor, king, and ruler
could not govern on heart & soul alone...

So I will venture where Caesar never dared,
I will equip for a battle that
Augustus never fared;
I'll turn a Dark Age into Palatine,
and I will build it
With Hardly a Dime.

But when I build it—
Will they come?
I'll stand by my Kingdom until
Kingdom come.

And should this forsaken fortress soon collapse:

My efforts will rebuild & double
&
I'll begin once again,
rebuilding from rubble.

CHAPTER 20

ART OF MIND II: ALL IN:
THE GALLERY (CONTINUED)

Rainy Romp

because Excessive Rainfall is more than an Umbrella
Term,
We'll rekindle and sear through this condition,
And we'll watch your umbrella burn.
We'll share the same cover and shield one another,
Let's prepare to storm through this weather,
One Umbrella is enough for us both:
We'll battle this squall together.
We won't sidestep the puddles of this downpour,
We'll strike down with a victory stomp,
We've overcome this Excessive Rainfall,
Now let's frolic in a Rainy Romp.

Painted by Chet Davis

Central Park South

Heading south are flights of traffic and birds; a single
pulse of the city in herds...There are motorists, cyclists,
aviators, and pedestrians...some moving in different
directions, but all under the same umbrella. Because in
this broad outlook of the city, there is only *one* umbrella.

There's an orange palm aglow, but in this city there is
no stopping. Only tracks to run around Great Lawns, a
Harlem Meer,
38 million a year cannot steer clear - -
We all fly like the birds and the Jets; pedestrians walk to
1st like the Mets...
Bikes await to stroll through Fifth Avenue,
And be met with speed long overdue.
This bustle was caused by hard hustle from pioneers who
cause jams like Russell.
This empire was built on
Capital and De Niro,
Gehrig, Mantle, and other heroes...
When the traffic backs up with red lights and too much
life for the roads to carry, but everyone seems to keep
charging anyway...either ride with us or move out the way,

I thought I told you that we won't stop.

Painted by Bruce Braithwaite

Box of Cretaceous

For centuries, man has quarried the strongbox of time—
not in chase of gold or fortune, wholly the valuable
commodity of unlocking the rotating vault. Archeologists
and Anthropologists have collapsed distance in order to
go back. Sages of science have examined artifacts dating
back to the pterosaurs while simultaneously seeking to
travel *through* the vault—where the hours seem to halt,
and our past and most lucid imaginations come alive and
transition our voyage to tomorrow. We await this hopeless
breakthrough left to the hands of cosmologists, wizards,
and rocket scientists...
While even a little girl in a blue nightie wandering in the
clouds—
Spellbindingly holds the key.

Painted by Vincent Cacciotti

Crimson Ballerina

When you step out there and move to the next stage,
Remember what you have learned; more importantly—
remember what you've displayed today.

Maintain a feminine form. Remind the world that they are
viewing art, not a performance.

Sustain a stable position. With your purpose and force
aplomb.

Always remain En avant, with the aid of your focus and
what's earned through discipline.

Be a danseuse of grace & poise. Let it blossom beside your
years.

When life goes down, up, down...maintain your balance
and step through it...with ladylike spring & elegance.

Give off the exterior of gliding...even when you are
tragically aware of your tumble.

Dance with your heart ouvert—soon, the right partner will
join you.

Ensure that your partner lifts you to breathtaking heights,
and is prepared to catch you on your land.

Live freely, but in Pointe Work: Stay on the Tips of Your Toes.

Take the cygnet of today and bloom into a Black Swan— but don't forget the Crimson Ballerina.

When you make it to the next stage,
Remember what you've displayed today...
In ventures of love, work, and art:

Always go All-In.

Painted by Kate Owens

PART 2

CHAPTER 21

HEART OF THE MATTER

Backflips Without the Show

That table with makeup is
Reserved for One,
I'll tell you a joke,
Then settle back down;
I would trapeze over tigers for you,
but
I Will Not Be Your Clown.

Heart of the Matter

She's got something inside that beats within me.
It sure beats being alone...
And it beats you, too.
Sorry. :0(

Not trying to break your heart, but...hmm...how do I
break this to you...
<snap>
You don't *have* a heart.

You've got a frame that could hang on the walls of horny
teenagers and grown men; legs that rise like Coconut
Pumps,
An ass built like a Dump Truck,
And a chest so big that it seems to have crushed your
heart.
What a Killer Smile.
You take wicked pleasure from the pain that you cause...
but then I remembered the one trait that you lack:
Your heart's broken.
Like a Female Dog who just Doesn't Give a Shit:
You're Housebroken.
See but *this* little lady is stronger than any Amazon,
Between you and her it's a No Contest:
It's her I've Already Betted On...
Because—
The heart doesn't matter to a woman like you;
&
The Heart of the Matter's she's more woman than you.

Tear Jerk

I am not here, My Dear, to console you,
What I want is to make you cry.
Go on. Cry for me.

Your tears are not a deluged bouquet of pain;
They are today's Spring from Yesterday's Downfall;
Allow me to soak it up—while it is still fresh.
This doleful resemblance is from a soulful remembrance:
Of the Bad Times, then the Good Times mixed with Ugly.
The larger fact is that there were times to be had.
For what is a man worth if no woman has ever cried for him?
I study the tears of damsels like a fascinated observer:
I am always gripped by what could cause such a collapse,
Then I consider *who* could cause the collapse:
Someone who once did something so very, very right—
before doing what feels so very wrong.
I've delved into the depths of my imagination:
And for the life of me I cannot imagine being on the other
side of the tears.
My entire life is filled with cries from being lovelorn,
For Once
I would like to be the grounds for mourn.
My appeal, though seemingly sadistic, is but a Hope of a
despondently Hopeless Romantic.
I do not want to take part in any drama,
I just wish to be the full brunt of your tragedy:

Just as Rhett Butler was to Scarlett O'Hara;
What Lancelot was for poor Elaine;

The Vronsky to your tormented Anna Karenina;

The Robert Lebrun to your Edna Pontellier...before she

swam out into the water. With the sea of your grief we will

rise like *Titanic* —

And die with names Entwined like Romeo & Juliet.

Go on, I said. Cry for me.

So that all audiences will feel your pain, share our story...

Then uncontrollably weep for Us.

CHAPTER 22

HUMAN PROWESS

Web

I'm entangled in the lacework of cobwebs in the small
corner of a dingy attic that is sealed for stretching
intervals—
While
You're caught in a web of lies.

We both deserve better.
I ought to be saved and you ought to be glazed—
In a sweeter love serum that consists not of the venom—
To which you've become immune.

Right when you're ready to escape, Daddy Long Legs
keeps tangling your thoughts with an interweaving of
toxin that makes you fall deeper...but it's not just *him* who
spouts venom—
You're toxic *together*...but you still deserve better.
And I deserve to be cut loose from this creepy attic and
crawl away from these cobwebs that haunt me so—but the
embedding of this netting lingers in my blood—My plasma
is coated in the splatter of refuse:

Now I'm a Brown Recluse.
Once more I hang above trapdoors—While you fall into
them...
I've felt the sting of regret—and you've been love bitten by
jumping spiders that can't stay in one nest—
But instead must Creep...
Some say love don't cost a thing,
He's shown that
Love is Cheap.

I think it's time you left him for dead—thereby making you
a Black Widow.
I'm not afraid that he's poisoned you against our kind—I
like 'em luscious & I like 'em lethal.
Love is dangling above us all,
Not this cheerful state of lust you call love...
I'm a man created to dwell in a True Love,
And you were made to star in a True Love Story:
Just let me cut you out of his web,
Then you can crawl right into my bed.

Maintenance

I've got to do some inside maintenance, before
I can even consider making a home.

I've got way too much junk in here, and although I could
use some company, I'm dreading the ringing of the
doorbell, because
I am Far From Ready to
Let Anyone In.
Fortunately, I'm not expecting anyone.
Unfortunately.

That gives me all the more time to clean up and get to
work...
On building a better me.

You can't expect someone else to clean up your own mess.

I've got to do some
Inside Maintenance,
Before I can even *think* about making a home.

I must roll up my sleeves and begin to seal the cracks that
go beyond my surface,
And repair the flood of thoughts that clog my future.
I'm drained—
and in desperate need of indoor plumbing.

Boy, do I have a lot of work to do...My soul leaks and everything is so damn drab and bland. I'm in need of an Extreme Makeover: Life Edition.

It's time to get to work.

When remodeling is complete and the doorbell sounds...
I'll happily let you inside—
And we can begin building a
Happy Home.

Human Prowess

The Date is booked.
Now I need to get ready.
Some don't have to. Their healthy genes provide them
with the right bone structure to help them grow and boost
strength without ever lifting a weight. Instead, they are *born*
with the ability to lift the weight Off Others—by making them
smile, making them laugh, and dropping off their presence.
Not Me.
If I want to get So Large I must train. I need to work to
have the ability to win this Grand Prize.
I want to be a Prize Fighter,
but I have some serious training to do.
I need to find
Sparring Partners to prepare me for my
Dream Match
I need to build up my
Social Stamina, Quick Witty Jabs, and People Skills - - -
Human Prowess.
Many others are naturally born with these attributes...they are
Born Alive.
I, however—
Have to get back in shape, so that I can put on a show—in
front of a Jam-Packed house of Two.

And in the unfortunate event that she's a No-Show,
Or we meet and I lose this battle...
It is my hope that after All My Training,

I'm fit to be someone else's prize.

CHAPTER 23

TOLERANCE

Elbow Grease

You're stuck,
but We don't have to be:
Just put in some
Elbow Grease.

If our status is in limbo it's because you're expecting
everything to
fall right into place, and for me to do all the heavy lifting...
but in order for us to pull this through:
We *both* need Elbow Grease to
spit-shine our path, then I can
Wax It.
Now we have a clean start, with possibilities
Wide Open—
but for us to release it all the way—
It will take the two of us,
not just me...
So let's pull together—
Beginning
on Three.

Loose

All I had to do was tap her from the back...
And out she came.

Yes, it took the right touch to make her love flow,
but I couldn't have done it alone. Bottled inside is a
torrent of emotion,
&
She's just dying to open up.

She hasn't always been this disclosing,
She was once wound as tight as a virgin,
Now she's ready to let her love spill—
Ever since *he* broke the seal.

And for That I should thank him.
Because some adventurers *can't* Travel Without Baggage.
So while it may seem too much for me to carry—
I should be grateful that it brought her to me.

Now we can celebrate her arrival in my life—
While waving goodbye to past lovers we won't see...
Like this Champagne—
She's quicker to Open Up—
After
He loosened her for me.

All I had to do was tap her on the shoulder—
And out she came.
She smiled and right then I felt welcomed.

Once I was a guest, now I'm prepared to buy the lease—
After she has let in So Many Prior Tenants—
My odds are most certain to increase.

My master key fits right into her hole—
No need to fumble or
Force my Hardened Key—
The hinges to her door spread
Willingly and Unhindered—
After
He loosened her for me.

For that I wish to shake his hand—
All while still
Rebuking his Name...
Once he was the Star in her Life—
Now he's *my* claim to fame.

So shake it up, babe, let me get inside...
Before I struggle, let's call a Loving Truce:

Open Up
&
Let's get Loose.

We are celebrating her arrival in my life—
While waving goodbye to past lovers
she won't see...
Like this Champagne,
She's quicker to Open Up—
After they loosened her for me.

Tolerance

Serve me the
Unadulterated Proof—
I am a Fully Grown Adult
In demand of your
Full Service.

I like my women how I like my coffee:
Black and Hot.
Better Yet,
I like my women how I like my whiskey:
Strong and Intoxicating.
I want to down *all* of your potency, but I fear that *you* fear
I'll find your undiluted nature to be impure.
So you save your strongest stuff for roughnecks at the
edge of the bar and discreet journeymen on the heels of
your confessionals.
Something tells me you think I am a lightweight because I
do not flaunt legendary stories of intake. But sweetheart,
believe me when I say:

You have No Idea how high my tolerance is.

No I will not judge, and I will not budge—
When I feel the effects of your
Absolute Content.

So here's to a raunchy good time...

Bottoms Up.

CHAPTER 24

WANTED

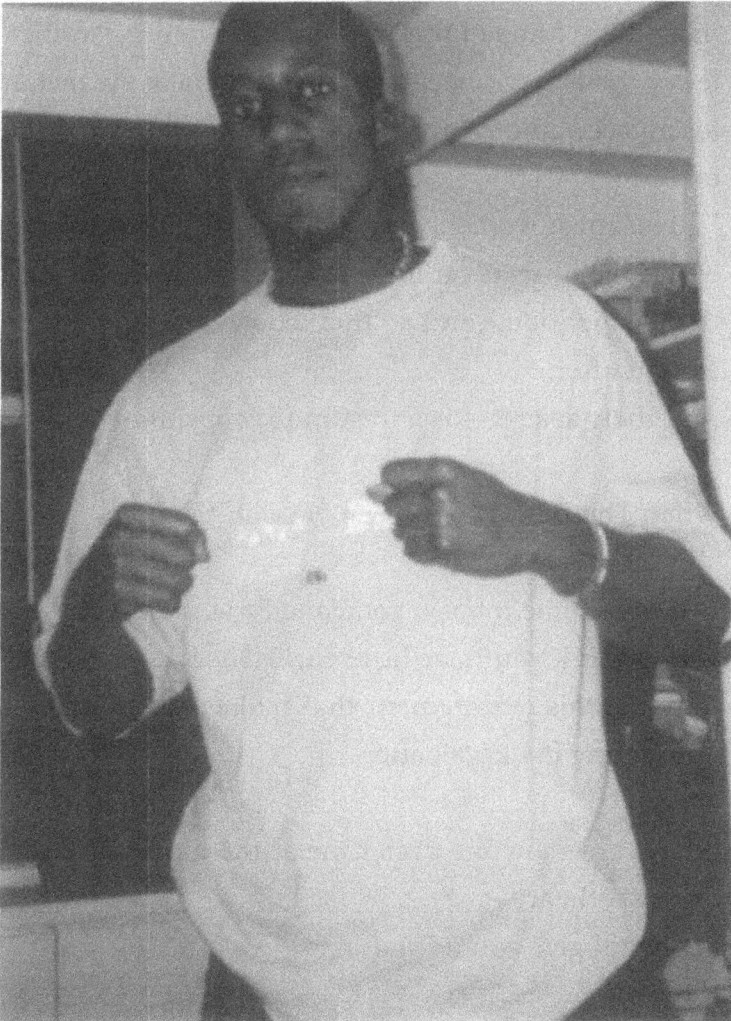

The Vacancy

This is a perfect fit.
I'm going for it.

What I like about this opportunity—is that there is so
much room for growth—and I can see my tenure spanning
a lifetime.
I know many have already held this position...but like
most men: I hope not *too many* have had it...in fact the
fewer the better...because I want to make my own name
for myself...and earn a distinguished place from the
others.
I guess most women view it differently. They want records
of past conquests on file—so that they can say they beat
the competition...and so they know their position is highly
sought after.
And their desire grows to gain this position—

When The Boss Has Proven He Can Succeed.

But to become a boss, someone First must believe in
you...even if you have little experience.
And it is *this* requirement that makes me second guess
submitting my application.

I don't have anyone under me at the moment...
but sweetheart—
I can still give you a Big Raise.

Don't be fooled by my inactivity...I may be out of business at the moment, but with *one* partner we can Create a Cartel.

It's hard to get a call back—when they suspect you don't have many references. Not too many can vouch for me... but what does that have to do with *this* opportunity? I do believe a fresh start is in order;

I'm loyal, dependable, and willing to work through nights...and Rise Again at the Crack of Dawn.

I need patience, understanding, faith...I also request many long hours.

I put on my sharpest suit and arrive at the interview...
I look her square in the eyes, and tell her why I am her man...
And assure her that I won't be deterred...
Then I hope to turn her rigid
"Experience Required,"
to a more flexible
"Experience Preferred."

Wanted

The rising sun casts a brooding foreshadow over this calm
western scene.
The hemisphere rests with the quiet breeze and brown
tumbling weeds
as the region wakes and grooms for saloons as the dusty
roads currently remain still.
It's a local peaceful.
About to be branded with chrome—of the cold steel of
roaming alone.

I'm an Outlaw—
Oh, you didn't know?
You better ask somebody,
I've got a body of work
That could shake somebody...
Yet whenever I shoot from the hip—
My targets just give me the slip.
I've got this need to be wanted, it's in my blood, it's in my
bones...
With all the damage I've done—
My name should have moved through homes.

Even the Greatest of Men have needed to be wanted—If
not by a lady, then by a group; if not by a groupie, then by
a lady.
It's a label we each deserve, but instead of being wanted—
some remain unclaimed.

I cannot reward you a fortune, I just want to be wanted.

I'm eluding capture like Jesse James, yet still going down
in flames—I cannot finger one culprit—
As No One is to blame.

I am not demanding or expecting a search party—
Just recognize who I am;
Please
Recognize what I've done.

Nor Am I awaiting a loaded cavalry:
Just One.
Anyone.

I am a fresh-faced bearded journeyman who takes refuge
in the corner of a bustling tavern. Drowning in bottle after
bottle, willing to tell my tales to you strangers—of how I've
eluded capture.

I wait for my billboard, poster, or composite sketch...
But they won't even give me a *Sign*

I just want to be wanted—and for the word to be attached
to my name. I want to be missed if I'm gone tomorrow,
searched for when I'm here today—without any place to
hide:

Wanted: Dead or Alive.

CHAPTER 25

NAPALM BOMBS

Yo, You Need to Watch Your Tone

You need to watch your tone. No, no, I didn't mean it that
way! Argh...now you see what I mean??
One misunderstanding leads to another—
Next thing you know you're trying to Kill Each Other.
Sarcastics get,
"Don't get smart with me!"
Shouters hear,
"Don't get loud with me!"
My tone is often Death Itself,
So I should hear,
"Don't Die On Me!"
Ah, but nobody'd care if I dropped dead—
Musta been Something I Said.

Seriously, though—watch your tone...
If you don't—a simple joke might not just stink—
but the room may go from
Silent to Deadly.
From personal experience I can tell you that being
misunderstood can be caused single-handedly by a

harmless joke being taken the wrong way. But if my tone
is death—then what's harmless to me may sound like me
wishing death on them...to them...
You still with me?
This applies to you, too...
The difference between being Loved or Hated,
Embraced or Chased,
Found utterly annoying or celebrated like I-Hop:
Is the ability to tell a joke.
The humor of the chastised comes from the same place as
the recognized—
It just gets distorted along the way...
by wit, timing, and most of all: tone.
I've both felt and witnessed what misplaced humor can
instigate. Do you not like "him" or just his jokes? Would
it matter if he always said, "Just kidding" or by then is it
already too late—
And you already made up your mind?

I wouldn't be surprised if every conflict the world has ever
had started with a joke being taken the wrong way.
While being dragged by a chain to the neck after being
stripped of all clothes and dignity, the first slave probably
said to his master,
"Come on, Dawg, I was just *playin!*"
Next thing we knew those chains were linked to over 500
years...
That musta been the Holocaust of jokes.
Speaking of the Holocaust, maybe a large group of Jewish
high school teenagers saw Hitler stepping out of an ice
cream shop, and one said,

"Bro, you've got... <gestures to upper lip> you've got some shit on your lip."
Then as Hitler touched his lip only to feel his shitty mustache, the group exploded in laughter before walking off. And as Hitler boiled with rage, he swore to himself, "I'm gonna get them!!"
Who knew that by "them" he meant
6 Million People?
Think about it, why else would crimes against humanity like these happen—
With No Provocation?
It's the best explanation *I* can think of.
Just as Adam eating the apple came back to bite all of us—
Maybe that first American slave saying,
"How long does it take for a white woman to take a crap?
......
9 Months"—was another human undoing.
And as all the homies was bustin' up,
The whities vowed revenge...
And that they Bet' not look at their women again after that joke.
If they did they'd end up like Emmett Till.
And when an onlooker said to the offended master,
"Come on, Lighten Up,"
He prolly took that wrong, too, cuz he was already White Enough.
Well, *I* don't want to cause no wars or racial subjugation or heinous genocides...hell, I'm like Tina, I don't really want to fight no more...so maybe I just won't say ish instead of stepping in shit—

You get me?

Even tight friendships unravel from jokes said in bad
taste,
You were expecting a laugh, instead got a punch in the
face—
So
Watch Your Step,
Watch Your Tone,
or else please
Watch Your Ass—
Or what you *think* are harmless words
May very well be your last.

LBVS.

It's Funny Because It's True

If you want to make a white crowd laugh, just tell them a joke about your being black...

It kills every time.

Napalm Bombs

They droppin' N Bombs like Napalm,
It Sticks on their Lips like Sticks of Lip Balm.
Oh, how we ran when we heard the bomb. We ran for
generations...centuries, even...until we caught up with
them.
Dream Realized.
Then we began to use the bomb ourselves, since it no
longer held the same threat...but unbeknownst to so
many in our culture...

It still holds the same power.

Run, Run.
Not for the fear of losing life but rather common sense.
We've seemed to have fallen behind even in the light of our
nation's president and all our progress if after all these
years of using their weapon,

We still don't Fucking get it.

It's *their* weapon.
Not a revamped gadget for our own amusement or a
harmless device of unison.
It isn't a code of Brotherhood,
It's the very same bomb that demeaned our Manhood.

Run! Run!

Because now Everybody has the bomb!

And now we can't cry foul...

Because we gave it to them.

So just

Run, Run...

We made it to Middle America,

but still we insist on staying in The Boondocks.

Run, brother. Run.

CHAPTER 26

KARMA INTERNATIONAL

Flybird

Right-on-Left
Right-on-Left
Right-on-Left–Right-Left...
Left....
Left.....
Left.....
I-Left - - -

On another march,
Three months past March,
In a Parade of One,
An Army of 1,
My uniform was a
Plain Blue-T-I-Think
With Blue Jeans
&
My own dark cloud
as Sunscreen,
Knaa'Mean?//
The setting was deep-tinged and tame—

Like a mild sun in Maine,
Felt of Hazels and Dew
on a swing of nothing new.
When I parked and had a seat—
That's when I held the Lorikeet.

Lasted all of six seconds,
But I held on to that tinted grin,
Shaped as fly as her colors,
And I never saw her again.

Karma International: A What Goes Around Comes Around Airline

This late May 1st evening,
Just blossomed a World Breaking New Ground.
Our Nation Rises as One:
'Cause we just got some new fertilizer.

Nine and about three quarter years,
Approximately THREE-THOUSAND-FIVE-HUNDRED
DAYS,
After an innumerable amount of tears,
and far too many graves,
We can hold our flags to our breasts,
And hear Obama say:
WE GOT HIS ASS!

Well...said in so many eloquent words,
It's a moment that is fond to
All who have served.
And to this proud nation who had their backs,
from this *essential* fight
to the War in Iraq.

Finally the day many thought we'd never see—
Has come to pass: Making History.

September 11th will never be forgotten,
From that day forward we *refused* to deter...
Well now we can add May 1st—
To the dates we recall where we were.

Earlier I was strolling outside...
I got caught in the
Suburban Spring Breeze,
Now I'm inside in this very proud moment:
Celebrating by stroking these keys.

I'm celebrating the only way I know how:
So here's to the troops who will feast at chow.
We'll be here rejoicing with you,
The following day: for the red, white, & blue.

And for the fallen soldiers who won't be in attendance,
For all the victims of that wicked plot,
I'll take this final drink with you:
Tonight, My Brothers:
We got the Last Shot.

CHAPTER 27

ADDRESSED TO THE PEOPLE
WHO CAN'T ADDRESS IT

Permanent Ink

I let them under my skin, but their names remain a
mystery...Have you ever wondered why when I write:
I Refuse to Use Permanent Ink?

I've been plugged by sharp needles from prick-happy
bloodsuckers many times, with wounds that refuse to
heal after 2-4 weeks. It festers like a scalding infection...
they mark me up—carving their names in my flesh...but I
refuse to carve their names in my books...

No, I don't do Permanent Ink.

So bleed me up again. Do your worst. I'll be sure to give
you dishonorable mention...In my latest cryptic verse.

I've also been inspired by sweet ass designs that caused
me to take my pen and write odes and tributes...and if I
dedicated a piece to anyone in particular:

I did it without Permanent Ink.

Because who knows if she'd care upon sight? More importantly, who knows if she'd care years later? And even if I won her with my words...and even if we ended up saying our nuptials...I've seen more than enough regretful faces that've
Gotten Names Removed:
For me to *ever* use Permanent Ink.

Addressed to the People Who Can't Address It

The handicapped can't write love poems.
Specifically poems of Unrequited love.
By "can't," that is not to say that they "can't..." but it is
just to say that the medically impaired aren't cleared to
walk with beauty queens.
Don't hate the judges,
Hate the pageant.
Then, to speak mournfully of love is expected, but the
outcome of their failed conquests is even more so.
For the disabled and damaged to speak ill of the *live*
or even with the slightest hint of derision upon their
foreordained decision—is to falsely represent oneself as
just another overlooked contestant—
When they know full well they were too broken to even
make it to the stage.

Don't hate the judges,
Hate the pageant.

If the disabled ought write an unrequited love letter, they
should address it to God like Celie,
The happy and healthy shouldn't be hampered with guilt,
They merit the gift to
Walk and Live Freely;
If a disability has anonymously robbed me,
While I thought the culprit was this world's pageantry,
Then my entire career of letters
Has been stamped with futility.

*A Diary of a Quasi-Poem Written Years Before You Are
Reading This*

If the world or I should end before this sees light—
I hope Heaven can see this trilogy—
I hope to take
Every Word
with me.

CHAPTER 28

FINAL SUPPER

Misplaced Faith

The body is a temple.
One that you were born into. But *of course* you were born
into it. Although Spiritual Births are not always pro-
choice, more often than not people are brought into their
realm—ready or not.
Scriptures of the Afterlife beget Pro-Life, and when
abortive measures are taken against their appointed
church, they are condemned to eternal damnation...or a
lower class in the next life...

Depending on where you were born.

Well, that's enough to make a believer out of many.
Even if in their doctrine they can find many flaws...
so they worship in accordance to location...
and work tirelessly to cleanse out their flaws.

If you're from the West you may seek to go to Heaven,
if you're from the East—you'd instead pursue Nirvana.
If from Jerusalem you may ask Rabbis for guidance,

if Korea you may find the Dalai Lama.

Who do you believe in?
What do you believe in?
Let me remind you that your body is a temple.
Who, oh Who: Will you let in?

Everyone has potential followers, but like every holy
sanctum: veneration is adverse to acclimation. Religion
is only two letters away from Region, which is why the
two are so close together. You may find someone who in
fact worships you...as do you him or her...but the faith
you share that your love is the truth, is a testament to
Position—not necessarily a Pious Movement.

If love were a Jehovah's Witness, it would be right outside
your door, but your prophet may be hundreds of miles
away...
Don't shoot the messenger.

Listen to your heart for the gospel of romance, and if it
tells you that your delivery is far, far away...
Go on a Pilgrimage—
to
Retrieve it.

The Grievance

The saddest part about death—
Is that life goes on.

The Grievance

***

The saddest part about death—
Is that life goes on.
Heads bow for a moment of silence.

Then the organ plays.

Just a moment.
That doesn't seem right.

One's lifetime is meant to rise above This prone figure and
Transcend the limp limbs that submissively embrace mortality.
They should look down on a life's work of love and behold
a reflection of themselves—among the living that *share*
what they see:
A Lasting Legacy.
With tributes and praises that continue longer than any
eulogy and Years after the
mourners have departed.

Instead, the memories bleed out for weeks, months,
maybe years onto diaries and the blank pages that are
conversations of remembrance...recorded in living souls—

Until the tears run dry.
Then smiles and laughter mock the deceased with carelessness...by walking past their graves to begin writing their *own* headstones.

Yet the dead smile anyway.

Because when monetary value and ambition don't pass through to the next life:

All that's left is Love.

So the deceased can rejoice that they are forgotten for hours, days, or even weeks at a time. They'd *want* the flower-givers to keep on walking...and begin that work on their own headstones.

You can't make a monument out of tears.

Besides, photographs in the memory album endure...even when laughter makes it seem like we've forgotten.

And should you feel guilty for reliving joy too soon... Remember it's exactly what they would want.

The happiest part about death—
Is that
Life goes on.

Amen.

The Final Supper

The table is set
for the grandest of pictures.
A Banquet arranged and yielding for masses.
Come as you are
&
Extend the Invitation:
&
Let this be the Final Supper.

***

Gates of Pearl open onto a spread
for
Kings and Merchants;
Beggars & Sages;
Wayfarers and Neighbors;
Yesterday & This Present—
a gift of provisions and sustenance...
of *Life*
Breathed into this vision of a large gathering with a bigger
meaning—
A Divine Purpose...
To put grief & beef aside to eat meat and meet on the
same floor—
A Common Ground.
Where Swastikas & Hebrews can Cross...
and learn to Compromise—for a Change.

Where white sheets are removed and not set aside but
thrown outside
to look a Brother in the face long enough to say Grace.

Let Us Hold Hands.

And sit still without movement to pass on this
magnanimous
Peace & Love Movement
to this generation and
On to the Next One
So that a newfound baby boy
Won't become a Lost Son.
Let's break bread and come together—
Savor this Delightful Occasion...
For even if not a single smile can be detected,
We're all sitting together
&
That's Progress Enough.

***

If the final hour was known and our final fates were
written on the winding clock of a predestined deadly
device...would we assemble, or fall apart? Would
impending doom of death set hatred aside...or would it
take the opposite? New Life?

As glasses of wine and bits of mutton are lifted and
greeted by happy lips,
I hover up above and wonder

If this could happen

If we each found a space:

In a much more Heavenly place.

Where evil can be stripped down to its roots.

Where Karma has *already* been served.

Where even the Sickest have had enough time to suffer...

Let this be our Very First Supper.

CHAPTER 29

GAMED LIKE A SILVER FOX

Man Down

"A man should accept his fate with dignity and courage."

This is a quote that has always stayed with me. The belief in this stoic adage has helped guide me through unbroken spells of disillusionment and obscurity. As the years of wasted youth warped into tasted truth—I've aged bitter like Chianti—
But I Refuse to Wine.
I won't waiver when surrender is invited—
I Will Choose to Grind.
Manhood isn't found on blocks, swaps, or gratified twats...
Even the most maidenly hunter can Pluck a Berry.

Too many detour from rocky roads but still claim to be rebels;
Dude, you *do not* have Big Stones,
You've got Fruity Pebbles.

Tales and miles on the meter of my travels remain untapped—but the motor that sustains me is Legendary.

Whatever will be—
Will Be,
The bull in the corner—
Is Me.
The true excerpt of manhood:
"He fights,"
To struggle with zeal
Is our passage of rights.

Note these words from a fallen soldier—
Enshrine them like a Shakespeare Sonnet...
I didn't claim to write the book on Manhood;

I just wrote the poem on it.

Gamed Like a Silver Fox

Slam me to the green—
Face Down—
On the Turf; I'll tackle the pain
and
Sack the struggle...
Don't be afraid to hit harder,
I welcome the pain,
I *need* the struggle.

Yeah, I'll avoid the rush, then weave through traffic...
But it's inevitable:
We All Get Hit.
Leave that Stretcher,
Remove your hands from your mouths:

Motherfucker I Live For This.

***

Chicago, IL
31°
Clear

Span the field.
Brace for the aural impact of cracked ligaments and
chill-building screams of 12th men now while you can as
the stands are still empty, for now—there is peace. Talk,
Tailgating, and Time are all that separate men of iron with
bad intentions and summoning annals of history that

ranges from benchwarming forgottens to the most durable of immortals: Iron Men.

Thousands of men have raced out that tunnel and took to the field only to taste grass, spit it out, lick their chops and get back up. But only *one* did it 321 consecutive times.

And it is *that* fortitude and grizzled tenacity

that drives me in battles much more

clouded in fog

than any of these people can see on this clear fall afternoon.

It is also the same fortitude that drives me when *I* take the field.

It is true that I have never strapped on a helmet and pads...but when I play: I go full contact.

Some guys take pickup games more seriously than Mike Singletary on Meth...I'm one of them.

Many men, even pros, escape larger battles by taking the field: I'm on that team.

The same Nordic mettle that allows me to take savage collisions and stand back up is the same toughness I carry day to day—day by day.

I like the pain. I welcome it.

Without it, I'd have nothing to get back up *from*.

I would stand

Shielded.

Untested.

Unchallenged.

No, sir, I told you

I welcome the blades,

I'm a Viking of an off-shade,

a Jet-Setter who is self-made,

I ain't Packing a damn thing, I'm right here in the pocket...

And

I won't run from an oncoming blitz...

I'll look the biggest brute dead in the eye:

And Welcome Another Hit.

The Pantheon

<Set to the Melody of "The Equalizer" by Sam Spence>

Cue the background music from NFL Films and
watch a craftsman do his work in a field flooded with
competitors—all clawing for acclaim—each chasing a
prize.
It's a game of courage, with men of skill or honor going
against something larger than themselves—often in
pursuit of themselves.
I jog out with helmet on and chinstrap hanging down with
an enthusiastic smile on my face—excited to take part and
compete.
I snap on my chinstrap and prepare for the ceremony...
Failure isn't shameful—it's a rite of passage...
Into a Pantheon of Great Men who climb to join the Mount
Rushmore of Drydens, Popes, and Hugheses—even though
those names are already *Etched* into the annals as the
all-time greats.
We still compete for the love of the field...or at least *I* do.
My stats read:

Over 350 Poems,
Countless Hours,
3 All-Star Books
Completed in
3 Consecutive Years...
All in my prime.

But I don't want to be remembered for poems complete or winning books...but for the genuine love of the craft—and the realness of every word I wrote.

And it is my honor to join the millions in this Pantheon of no-names...

Because the very fact that my name is listed—

Puts me in the Hall of Fame.

CHAPTER 30

IRON MAN

6/23/11 13:00

<Set to the Melody of "WWE Dreamchild" Instrumental>

Since the age of 12, it has possessed him, haunted him,
Made Him What He Is Today.

The young child, now a man, still consumed by the
Undying Dream.

Day after day.
Week after week.
Year.
After
Endless Year.

In the Iron Man Poem, one unforgettable piece will define
a lifetime of yearning.

What becomes of the man...when he finally fulfills his dream?

What becomes of the boy...if he doesn't?

Iron Man

"I will give you a show like you have never, *ever* seen
before. Why? Because I can."

—   "The Heartbreak Kid" Shawn Michaels

Wrestlemania XII featured what was called an "Iron
Man Match." It was designed as a 60-minute marathon
match without interruption for the World Heavyweight
Championship. The winner would be the competitor who
scored the most pinfalls in the time allotted. The bout was
between the champion, Bret "The Hitman" Hart, and the
challenger, "The Heartbreak Kid" Shawn Michaels.

Shawn Michaels was my childhood hero. Every kid
needs figures to look up to, and for me, no one was more
worthy than Shawn Michaels. People get so caught up in
wrestling being scripted or "fake" that they often overlook
the larger-than-life individuals that appear on televisions
across more than 145 countries. Men just as large as
Sylvester Stallone or John Wayne are in fight scenes not
once a year or every few years, but every single week—
with contact *much* more realistic.

And with every star doing his own stunts.

The reasons for Shawn Michaels being my childhood hero
are plenty. He was the most entertaining character—with
a persona filled with charisma and accessibility. Michaels
always seemed to be the easiest wrestler to connect to as
either a good guy or a villain. He was so quick, athletic,

and talented...and what I liked most about him was that his character displayed more heart than anyone else.

I was always the smallest kid in school, and watching Shawn Michaels inspired me by proving that you don't need to be big to stand up to larger foes. He showed that with savvy, speed, and heart, you can keep getting back up and kick the world in the face before having your hand raised in victory. And even when you lose, you still find the strength to return the following week ready to get clobbered again, only to keep getting back up.

I truly believe that Michaels was better at portraying that character than Sylvester Stallone ever was. The Rocky Balboa character provided the template for such a character, and as such—the character is immortalized not only within me, but millions around the world. Michaels, though, depicted it in a more lifelike environment, where personas and the actual portrayers are much more linked, and therefore fans form a stronger bond to the *man* as much as the character.

The Iron Man Match was the culmination of the Shawn Michaels character. The character who was told he couldn't make it. Who was told he was too small, even though he was the most talented and worked the hardest. The match was hyped as a man chasing his boyhood dream. I can still remember the "Dreamchild" promo videos leading up to *Wrestlemania XII*, describing Shawn's journey leading up to this moment. I felt his *real* passion and I shared the dream. And it was around this time, that I subconsciously knew that I too had to have my own dream—my own "impossible" ladder to climb. When *Wrestlemania XII* finally arrived, I witnessed Shawn Michaels win the World Title for the first time ever. "A boyhood dream come true." A joy shared by myself and all of his millions of fans throughout the world. It was here when I decided that in some way and some fashion, I was going to chase my own dream, and I would welcome a grueling, never-ending journey that drains everything from inside of me in order to realize it.

***

Round 1

6/25: Art of Mind Arena

Today is a monumental event:
But I'm hosting an
Audience of One
Come join me in a Final Celebration:
The show has just begun.

Here today we have booked a marathon display:
One Man,
24 Hours,
Come witness a lone spade parade:

I've nested in black holes too deep for raiders,
and managed to claw my way out
without a flashlight, but rather a headlight that stemmed
from inside the very brain
that could diagnose a lesser man as
Clinically Insane.

Now I see the Sun.

But it's still the same day.
An ordinary date for the rest of America,
But one I hope to become a holiday.

I'll get to that a little bit later.
But first I have a story to tell.
This one will be quite long,

I'll do my best to tell it well.

On a hot July Chicago night
A child was born.

The End.

The truth is there wasn't much of a story to tell,
But see, I went and told it anyway.
Because I believe that no matter how obscure or buried:
Everybody has Something to Say.

So these volumes of painkillers and
Methadone Thrillers
That have helped me cope with the slack of life's rope
Is dedicated to a nation of odd birds:
It's
For Those Who Can't Find the Words

Because
It Only Takes One Time
To claw your way out.
&
It Only Takes One Time
To dig someone out.
Yes, and it only takes one time to reach above,
Just as it
Only Takes One Time
to
Find Love.

So many are having dirt kicked on them far too many
times as they are *still* awaiting rescue.
When the whole world continues to trample over you
without even noticing your plight,
Remember these Words:
Anyone can be found...
Yes, even
In the Suburbs.

While awaiting rescue it's only natural to set up a
workshop
and learn to create language with so much strength
that you're appointed the power to legally change your
name—
from a John Doe Stoic
to a
Mr. Poet.
And it is this New Self that serves as a companion to the
Former One,
And it is this outlet that helps you unplug the day...with
the inspiration
to see Another One.

When the circles you want to enter have
Capacity Met
Do not sit in your bed and moan:
"If you can't find your place in the world,
You have to make your own."
That, my friends, is the
Outsider's Mantra.
It has served me well

Like Frank Sinatra.
Because even if I died today:
I'll know I did it my way.

I have bled for strangers without expecting any help,
And I'd do it all again.
I've spoken unfiltered with the previously untapped clarity
of freshwater oceans with a collection as wide as the Baltic
Sea and as Open as the Land of the Free.

I've held my hand to my heart and I've sung like a fucking
canary.
In return, I received immunity...and have been released,
yes
Now I'm Free.
No longer in that same dark hole.
Though
Still in Solitary.

For Artists are solitary beings,
Whether a lady spinster or family man...
Because there is an art that they can't bring out:
You must venture solo to see that Only You Can.

Disappointments have fried souls raw and left you a cold
plate of hash reality.
That's Harsh.
Kinda leaves you with a bitter aftertaste du'nit?
Caffeine Dreams run on empty,
Wash it down with the tears that've been brewing for years
from the freshest ingredients of pain, stained with the

Blood, Sweat and Tears of loves of Yesteryears who went
on their merry way, while you're left with the cost
&
Stuck to Pay.

It's okay,
You'll be back tomorrow,
After waking up in a
Bed of Clichés,
And hopefully you'll dine well on the dish of revenge—
served up best by Living Well.

Feasting on Vultures? Now That's the Spirit!

Now that cold plate is filled with their hate.
Let it consume you to motivate you:
To make *sure* they don't forget about you.

Round 2

Hello, good morning,
How's it going?
That's about the extent of my social contribution today.
If you want to know my innermost thoughts.
Yes, I'm afraid you'll have to pay.

Though I promise to charge the minimum amount,
I realize I have *The Gift*
So Remember:
It *is* the "Thought that Counts."

I dread and loathe small talk,
Which is why I prefer to give long lectures,
So go on, Wave to the Professor!
While I'm giving critics lewd gestures.

The forecast on this June day is partly cloudy. There
is minimal inpouring with No Signs of Rain. Ten years
from now it may be storming...But who knows what the
forecast will be that far in the future?

My complaints are growing fewer and fewer,
I just hold the days in my hands like a hornet holds
honey,
Then I take my pen
&
Bleed it Dry.

80 percent of us know what it's like to be strange.

And we All have felt discarded.

We take part in Great Diversions:

In a Grand Hoax that should be Applauded.

We mute voices that speak

Universal Truths,

Funny jokes are told to hide Real Meaning,

We adorn

Sick Senses of Fashion to dress up the world's

imaginations to complement

Our Views of Ourselves rather than How We Really Look.

This isn't a message to take off the makeup,

No, Baby, Leave It On!

The world could use more superstars.

And we could all

Use My Imagination:

Where everything about us doesn't *need* to be known,

It's the child of mystery

That can thrive when it's grown.

And now I'm making a *formal* request to pick up a semi-

lady of the evening wearing the most inappropriate dress

and take her to balls.

Then I want to mingle with Porn Stars

and verbally dance with flirts until I get underneath their

skirts...

Then toast to a wonderful evening, saying, "Cheers to the

Memories."

It's OK to imagine a girl who smiles like Gabrielle Union

and

Fucks like Annette Schwarz.

It's that combination of classy and nasty that many
women try to master,

but only a few perfect. But I've noticed that the girls who
fearlessly share that Very Same nasty side with the *world* with
less fear of being judged are indeed more likely to become
impregnated, but the world is even more likely to breed
Promiscuous Birth

The umbilical cord of hate is slammed into Rainbow
Brides, Porn Stars, and women who are guilty of only
being extra friendly without the cord around their neck
seemingly ever being cut off.

Let them be.

There's no place to condemn a man for fucking a man or
a woman for fucking a thousand men...these are acts that
we need not forgive.

I stand by a famous, common creed:

We should all

Live and Let Live.

It's natural to have opinions and disagreements,

But in the end we can make our own choices.

Yes, we are *all* created equal.

Whether or not we agree with others' choices.

Now, more than ever, we have the power to connect.

This huge globe can be covered within an iPad screen.

We can see and celebrate our differences,

Perfect Strangers can meet and convene:
To create a Magical Box with just the right tools to plow
through our
Walls and build *real* friendships based on
Two Characters
With
No Word Limit,
With connections built wider than any city limit:
Alabama, New York, or Tennessee:
"If you are a man in need,
I'll be a friend indeed."
&
"If you need a friend and peer,
Just know Da Champ is here."

I don't write empty verses, I'm all too aware of all the
Other 1s who *still* can't find the words, and it is with
the Deepest Apologies if I am unable to find or catch your
waterfalls...
But if you can find *me*,
You can call me anytime.
I mean it, just ask & I'll give you my number:
This isn't a "fitting rhyme."

We'll have *Good Times* and make our own *Saturday Night
Live*;
We'll
"Smile cheek to cheek."
&
The best part of it all:
We'd do it all again the next week.

Unfortunately, far too often the world isn't quite so lovey-dovey with such heartwarming albeit cliché sentiments.

Every day someone is spontaneously backed up over by someone they used to ride with...only now to be in their *Rearview*
And they're gone before you even have the chance to dust yourself off and wish them happiness.

Moreover, so many remain without company because they don't fit into the role society has cast for them...they continue to *dare* to color outside the Black & White lines of the world and the punishment is 180 discrimination with drive-bys of judgments from people who can't even show their *own true colors*...they're too busy riding the underground railroad. They hide behind the march of people doing the exact same things.

When we live in a world where we're all *clearly* born different, yet it's so hard to embrace others' differences...
Who needs pills to be Dazed and Confused?

Well, thank God for family,
Where we can say,
"They won't judge me."

My parents and siblings instilled love that has sprouted:
But my Expression has Developed Without It.

It's filled with recipes that were self-taught,
Created with the same passion that has got me by...

It's from the soul of a kid who evolved into a man,
With a nice, warm slice of
Humble Pie.

It takes more than affirmative action to bring all these
flavors together.
It takes the right touch of faith,
A precise amount of peace,
with only a tablespoon of love to work with.

Even if my words could bring people together or rewrite
a man's story or even make a lorikeet return to the palm
of my hand...at the end of the day, there will still be the
same injustices of the world. People will still be mugged...
murderers will still have love while many good guys
won't...and there will still be the unsolved mystery of what
decides who is happy or when one is happy or why there
are so many
Cold Case Files of missing people in so many unresolved
love lives.

And after I have brought all the colors in the world
together with feathers as varied as the lorikeet...and I've
held that kind of power in the palm of my hand...I'd still
end up returning to that empty atelier:

And I'd sit alone again.

Well,

Thank God for Headphones.

Round 3

I've hung out with M.J.
Yep, I've
Danced with Michael Jackson.
No, seriously, it's true. I've hung out with M.J.
And Sam Cooke, Elton John, Madonna, Stevie, Diana
Ross, John Lennon, Jimi Hendrix, Beyoncé, Kanye,
Aerosmith, Shakira, Pink, Jonny Lang, Sarah McLachlan,
Jack Johnson, Mariah Carey, Hall & Oates, Tenacious D,
Norah Jones, The Game, Linda Ronstadt, Gwen Stefani,
Muse...the King of R&B R. Kelly...hell, I've even
Ridden with the Eagles.

If it weren't for my headphones, I may not have had the
inspiration to write...
So thanks to All of Them, and *Hundreds* More: I've shared
my story.
And if you ever want to hear the passion that I write from:

Just Listen to a Rob Thomas Song.

Music is the gospel that renews spirits & faiths in
Churches of Love
across America.
Music helps to patch the wounds of
Broken Love,
When friendly remedies aren't enough.

It is the
Savior

of
the weak.
The humbler
Of the
Strong.
It is
Pure
The equalizer where the wealthy
Break Even with the Poor—
The only channel where we *all*
Envy the Blind:

Because they can hear much better than we do.

It's the escape where we can all drive to the moon...Where every last one of us can feel like Rock Stars.

We can book *Travel Arrangements* inside our own minds to be pleasantly stranded on an island with only a pair of headphones. Every zone I've felt is due in part to every song I've heard.

And I'm shaped at least a *little* by every purchased CD.

This *Writer Without a Cause* who in my own mind has built an Empire or at *least* a Kingdom...has had the help of a *Devil* Without A Cause and quite a few downloaded Princes.

I've welcomed being on fire. I just *Stop, Type and Roll* and burning a mother down for me is

Modus Operandi

One Minute
Becomes
2 Minutes,
Next thing I know
I'm staying in tonight.
And the next night,
And the next night,
And so on and so forth.

As I said before, artists are solitary beings...I only need a
pen, paper, and a pair of Headphones...

I've tried not to disappoint, but if I have...

I hold no regrets,

Because I know the place it all came from.

&

I am certain of what I have built.

But after *All These Words*...
After *All These Lines*...
Have I realized *my* Boyhood Dream?

Though my dream isn't what you might think it would be.

I've taken the most boring true story,

and completed an Immortal Trilogy.

But that was not my Dream.

Like that 12 year old boy, this man still yearns for love.

But finding it is not my dream.

Neither is fame, wealth, notoriety as a writer, or even the very concept of winning itself.

Since the age of 12, when I vicariously dreamed Shawn Michaels' dream, and in all likelihood, some years before that and every single day since...my dream has been to take everything thrown at me...and just like Shawn Michaels, just like Rocky Balboa, just like Brett Favre every time he was hit, just like Allen Iverson skidding on the basketball floor...

To get back up.

I imagined myself mounting a comeback just like HBK and yes, earning a victory...but even if I lost that would still be of the same value, but only in a different light. It would show how I would come back the next day stronger...or even weaker...but the point is: *I came back.*

Whenever I lay my head down after yet another empty, unfulfilled day, that's me going down for the count.

When I wake up, and I search for a reason to get up, I feel the referee holding my arm up...dropping it two times... and on the third drop, I hold my arm up...and I struggle back up to my feet.

My dream is to be *Gamed Like a Silver Fox*

To take the very best shot of

Rejection, Insecurities, Loneliness, Isolation, Demons, Heartbreaks, Punches, Kicks, Scrapes, and Bruises from sources Much Bigger Than Me:

And continue to get back up...much to the awe and shock of my imaginary audience. This entire series is built on delusions of grandeur,

But with the aid of The Greatest Art of All:

My dream has been realized since the age of 12.

And on 6/25 last year, I found the muse to celebrate it.
And on this one year anniversary:
Once again I encourage you all to celebrate your own.

As well as that of others.

I encourage you to
Share your Headphones,
but embrace your *own* art.

To develop a deeper appreciation on this day for everything from cinema to fine arts, music, paintings, thoughts, and any and all things Art.

I'd like to create an informal holiday:

Art Appreciation Day.

But of course I'd be foolish to think I, my words, or even the very place that it came from which I call to be celebrated has that kind of power. Which is why I'm prepared to continue hosting the
Audience of One as this show and this holiday comes to a close.

If it is any extra incentive to celebrate with me, just remember that arguably the Greatest Artist Who Ever Lived:

Coincidentally died on this very same day.

Tonight, and hopefully for all the days and years to come, I will depart from the atelier and *live*. Because it is long overdue. I will search for love with an open heart...and when I find it...

Don't be expecting me to come back writing love poems.

And should I fail, the question wouldn't become what happens to the boy if the dream isn't realized...it would become:

What happens to the boy...when after he's realized he's realized his dream...

The man realizes it isn't enough.

To which the answer is quickly supplied:

He'll keep getting up.

I got my black shirt ready and my white pants.

And my black & white "O.C.A." bracelet.

Yes, I'm tired of being stuck in this cave.

It's time to celebrate this holiday.

It's time to celebrate *life*.

***

I think I'll go out now.

THE END ☺

Painting Images

(TO SEE EACH IMAGE IN THIS BOOK AS WELL AS OTHER GREAT WORKS BY THESE ARTISTS IN FULL COLOR, PLEASE VISIT THEIR GREAT WEBSITES!!!!)

Websites of Other Great Artists of the Art of Mind Trilogy:

Robert Beck: www.robertbecknet
Vincent Cacciotti: www.vincentcacciotti.com
Yashmin Campagne: www.yashmincampagneart.com
Juliette Caron: www.juliettecaron.com
Joe Cartwright: www.joecartwright.com.au/
Daniel Colvin: www.colvinart.com
Chet Davis: www.artsites.org/ChetDavis
Judy Gilbert: www.creativitymindset.net/
Luis Ludzska: http://luis-ludzska.artistwebsites.com/
Donna Marsh: dmarsh.artspan.com
Cynthia McBride: www.hillismcbride.com
Aixa Oliveras: aixaoliveras.artspan.com
Minako Ota: www.minako-art.com
Kate Owens: www.kateowensstudio.com
Eric Palson: www.ericpalson.com
John Penney: http://www.artistjohn.co.uk/
Lori Pratico: www.loripratico.com
Bonnie Shapiro: www.bonnicshapiro.artspan.com
Kari Tirrell: www.karitirrell.com
Debi Watson: www.debiwatson.com

Special thanks to each of these great artists for lending their talents in support of this series, and a heartfelt thank you to each and every reader.